To. Lesley + Robbie.

Not my Book its Theodore's
But Next Year who know's
Hope you have a great Christmas
And a happy New year.
Dont ~~try~~ try these recipe's at home.
They don't work.

Cheer's.

Stuart.

P.s. Your daughter Can Cook.
Better than me. Even though she's
A Vegetarian

Look forward to See you Both
at Christmas.

the LIVEBAIT
cookbook

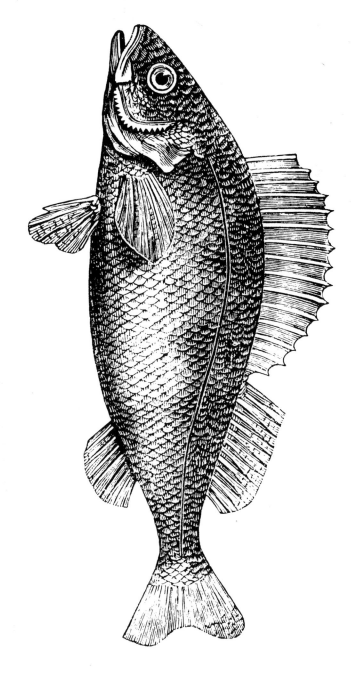

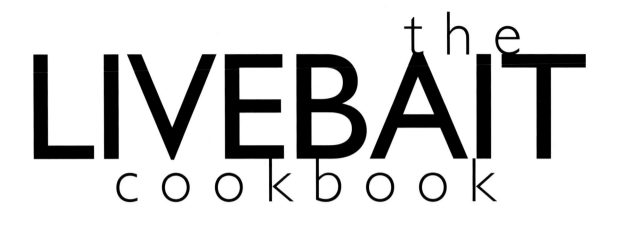

the LIVEBAIT cookbook

Theodore Kyriakou

and

Charles Campion

Hodder & Stoughton

Design: Isobel Gillan
Photography and styling: Sandra Lane

Hodder and Stoughton
A division of Hodder Headline PLC
338 Euston Road
London NW1 3BH

A Word of Thanks

It is only when you come to write a paragraph which thanks everyone for their help that you find out just what a team game writing cookbooks can be. With an apology in advance to all those who we have inadvertently omitted . . .

Thanks are due to the brigade in the Livebait Covent Garden kitchen, particularly Bridget Chick, Beatrice Ferrante, Yannick Tual, Michaela Beer, Matthew Laine, James Enrile, Alexander Carvajal, Patrick Jamleck Kiragu, Eric Mulundi, and Nick Brown for bearing up despite a lot more filleting, cooking and extra preparation work. Also to the managers and front-of-house staff: Paloma Santa Maria, Linda Miles, Justine Mclennan, Deborah Fellows, Emma Clyde, Lisa Stephenson, Sharon Fennell and Carlo Renzulli, for running a restaurant despite having someone writing in one corner, someone taking photographs in another, and all of it happening at lunch time! Also Mark Yates and Katrin Olander, without whom there would never have been a Livebait in the first place, and to Neville Abraham and Laurence Isaacson whose restaurant company Groupe Chez Gérard not only bought the original Livebait restaurant at Waterloo but had enough faith in the concept to create the new and large Livebait in Covent Garden. To Manu Feidel, Emma Scott and the team at Livebait Waterloo. To Susan Campbell, for tirelessly testing an endless succession of fish recipes, (usually against the clock). To Clayre Broadfield, for testing some of the other recipes. To Roland Philipps, Anna-Maria Watters and Hazel Orme at Hodder and Stoughton for putting up with weeks of, 'We'll be sending you some more manuscript soon.' Also to Isobel Gillan for laying out the book so elegantly, and Sandra Lane for her exceptional photographs. And, finally, to all the fish-loving customers who have made Livebait such a success.

Theodore Kyriakou and Charles Campion,
Livebait Covent Garden August 1998

Contents

A Surprise Around Every Corner

Charles Campion

My first visit to Livebait (which in those days was a small black and white tiled establishment, in a street named The Cut behind Waterloo Station) was a strange one. For a start it was four o'clock in the afternoon, and for another thing I was in the middle of a day-long oyster-eating marathon (one of the more enjoyable surveys I have undertaken for *ES*, the Friday magazine of the London *Evening Standard*). I reached Livebait with the first four dozen oysters under my belt, quite literally. As I walked in, Theodore looked me up and down and came out of the kitchen with a large basket of bread, and a pint of Guinness. The bread was amazing: there was a yellow-hearted loaf musty with turmeric, a dark one with flecks of olive, one bright red with smoky paprika – all were warm, all were delicious. Particularly to a passer-by who had spent the day sampling molluscs and so ingesting about a gallon of cold sea water. The oysters were good too, lovingly opened, carefully presented. So this was it, the fish restaurant everyone was talking about.

Then, as now, the Livebait speciality seemed to be an ability to cause the maximum amount of stir in the minimum amount of time. Livebait first opened its doors on 26 September 1995: the restaurant was a partnership between the chef Theodore Kyriakou, and Mark Yates and his fiancé Katrin Olander, who were responsible for the front-of-house. There were also two 'sleeping partners', Michael Wood and Mick Richards. The venture was a brave one by all concerned and had a good deal more enthusiasm behind it than hard cash – one of the reasons for the 'minimalist' design of the banquettes and the simple black and white tiling is that the partners built the seating and did all the initial painting and decorating themselves, anything much more complicated would probably have proved too costly.

Throughout the latter part of the 1990s any, and every, chic London restaurant would proudly allude to its philosophy, some even boasted written 'mission statements'. They all felt the need for a precise description of their food – 'Modern British', vying with 'Pacific Rim', 'Mediterranean' or 'Fusion'. Livebait has had no such formal straitjacket, but it has nurtured its own distinctive philosophy. What Theodore and his team have created is the ultimate in 'market-driven' restaurants: in Waterloo – and now in Covent Garden – the menu at Livebait changes daily, not in response to the latest fashions, not even in response to the whims of the head chef, but in response to the market. Having set out to buy only the best fish, who can tell what will be best later on in the week? Today there is a huge and beautifully fresh turbot, tomorrow (if most of today's customers are sensible enough to choose the turbot dish from

the menu) there will be no turbot to be had. The menu is constantly changing and always exciting, and Livebait regulars find themselves choosing confidently – exotic fish, innovative combinations, even dishes they have never heard of.

As any French chef will tell you (indeed, it is a subject any French chef will be delighted to lecture you on), British diners love the plain and unadventurous; lack discernment; and are hell to cook for. Then, reluctantly, Monsieur will go on to tell you that things in Britain 'may be getting a little better'. Livebait is one of the places where this improvement is most marked. In a country where fish is still viewed with suspicion, it is amazing to think that a restaurant can succeed by offering roast cod with butter bean and black pudding stew; or by serving nearly raw seared tuna; or by teaming monkfish and belly pork. Hurrah for the customers! The result of this open-mindedness has been a niche for Livebait, and acclaim as the most consistently innovative fish restaurant in Britain. It also means exciting dining. You might compare it to watching the final stages of a village cricket match, the blacksmith takes strike and swings wholeheartedly at every ball. Mostly he connects and the ball vanishes into the next parish for six, but occasionally he misses whereupon he is out. The important thing is that it is always exciting and never dull – the perfect summary of everything that is best about dining at Livebait.

As word of these strange combinations of fish and meat, or fish and shellfish, or simply of unheard-of exotic fish, started to leak out, London's restaurant critics – after the usual period spent squabbling over who was first to discover the place – gave Livebait better and better reviews. Awards followed, and by February 1997 Groupe Chez Gérard, a large restaurant company, stepped in with an offer to buy. (As Victor Kiam is so fond of saying in his television adverts, they 'liked the product so much they bought the company'!) For Neville Abraham and Laurence Isaacson of Groupe Chez Gérard, the Livebait concept represented something new and vital, and what was even more exciting it specialised in fish. Livebait made the perfect counterweight to their highly successful Chez Gérard chain which is renowned for paying homage to steak frîtes.

The challenge for Theodore Kyriakou was to take his personal and highly idiosyncratic style of cooking and make it work in a brand-new, larger restaurant over the river in Covent Garden. Theodore was born in Athens, where his parents ran a prosperous delicatessen and food shop. Some of his earliest memories are of long ferry trips with his father to purchase olives from producers scattered throughout the Greek islands. Or of making the yearly visit to buy the grapes, which were then to be shipped back to Athens to make wine for the family. For someone with such an early grounding in good food, it took him a very long time to find his way to a career in the kitchen.

Theodore left school for college to study for his exams in the Merchant Navy, and then for many years he criss-crossed the world's oceans as he worked his way up from third officer to second captain. After a couple of spells low on income but high on adrenaline, when

he volunteered his services for successive Greenpeace missions, he found himself in London looking around for a new career. Necessity meant that the kitchen finally beckoned. In 1988 he started working as a commis chef at Pollyanna's on Battersea Rise, London; by 1993 he had done stints as chef de partie under Dan Evans at the Fire Station restaurant in Waterloo, London, and with Fergus Henderson at St John in Clerkenwell, London. In 1994 he got his first job as a head chef at the Stepping Stone restaurant, Battersea Rise, London. A year later he had opened Livebait. A fairly meteoric assault, by any standards, upon what has recently become a competitive and glamorous profession.

For the opening of the new Livebait in Covent Garden, Theodore took the unusual decision to start with completely new kitchen staff, rather than leave the original restaurant with a parallel problem by moving his old brigade across the river. His problems were compounded by the arrangement of the kitchens at Wellington Street. The restaurant is within the building that houses the Lyceum theatre and a good many facilities must be shared. The main kitchen is deep within the bowels of the theatre and is linked by lift to a small open service kitchen at one end of the restaurant. The day's work starts down in the main

kitchen with all the preparation and then, just before the lunch rush starts, all the chefs troop upstairs to man the service kitchen where the dishes are cooked and finished. The same procedure is repeated each evening. Living cheek by jowl with the theatre has led to some amusing incidents, especially in the early days. Amid the flurry of opening parties and while working out how to get the best from various bits of new machinery, even the most saintly chefs can find their tempers fraying, and so it was that a message was bellowed down the intercom to a French kitchen porter – let's call him Pierre. 'Bring up the large cod, immediately' would give the meaning of his instructions, though not convey the vocabulary or urgency with which they were issued. Pierre duly snatched up a handsome 3 kg cod and bolted out the kitchen for the restaurant. But instead of turning left up

the stairs, he turned right through the swing doors deeper into the theatre, then the one-way doors promptly swung shut behind him. On he wandered until eventually he found himself back stage during a performance of *Jesus Christ Superstar*. By this time what little English he could speak had quite deserted him, leaving the theatre's front-of-house manager to telephone the restaurant and ask, 'Have you lost a small Frenchman with a large fish?'

There was also the unfortunate occasion when ghostly music could be heard during every lull in the performance. This was finally traced back to a chef's boogie box tuned to Kiss FM, which was echoing in the shaft of the food lift where it had been used as a makeshift doorstop.

When enthusing about the new Livebait restaurant during a television interview Laurence Isaacson said, 'We wanted it to be a more accessible kind of fish restaurant, where you can sit at the bar and enjoy a bottle of beer and half a dozen oysters, just as much as settling down to an elaborate three-course dinner.' And that's what Livebait has become, perhaps its greatest strength is that it is completely classless. Stylish, yes. Snobbish, no. Just like Theodore's recipes.

Most cooks would concede that they don't make as much use of fish as perhaps they should. We know that fish is good for us, but we're still scared of the bones and wedded to soggy fillets in batter. We are all guilty of underestimating and overlooking fish, despite knowing in our heart of hearts that it is a splendid natural food.

Diners at Livebait will tell you that fish can be made exciting, and Theodore's recipes will show you that exciting fish dishes are a lot easier than you think. Enjoy this book (and in the process eat a good deal more fish) – you'll find that there's a surprise around every corner.

surprise

'Fish tales' – an early-morning stroll through Billingsgate fish market

C.C. *There's no doubt about it, 4.30 a.m. is very early indeed, but the market is just beginning to buzz. Are you a regular visitor to Billingsgate?*

T.K. To tell you the truth, I have never been before. At Livebait we are always trying to work our way back up the supply chain, because that means fresher fish and a better choice. Rather than buy from a wholesaler – who buys from a Billingsgate dealer, who in turn buys from a trawler's agent – we like to buy direct from the boat. It can mean that we get our fish as much as forty-eight hours fresher. Of course, all the overseas and exotic fish comes in by air freight, but for these we try to deal with the shipper rather than the wholesaler whenever possible. Most of our inshore fish comes up from Poole harbour in Dorset, and we also get a lot from Guernsey – the waters are very clean around the Channel Islands.

So as Billingsgate is new to you, what are your first impressions?
To be honest, I'm surprised by how small it is. When I worked on the Continent I grew to love the huge fish markets. Even middling towns would have a good-sized fish market, and in cities like Barcelona and Paris they are many times the size of Billingsgate. For a people surrounded by a sea full of fresh fish, Brits are remarkably wary of eating them. You'll notice that, aside from the trade, a good many of the members of the public buying fish here are Chinese. That's a good sign, the Chinese love fish but it has to be fresh – they also relish a bargain.

What's your favourite fish?
John Dory. And I'm not just saying that because there's a magnificent one just over there! The John Dory has the perfect combination of firm flesh and a delicate flavour, which means that you can do so much with it.

12

So how can you tell when you're getting really fresh fish?

Well, it's time to go on the offensive. Ask your fishmonger, or the person behind the fish counter in the supermarket when they took delivery of their stock. Sometimes this may force them to lie to you, but however good or bad we are at judging the freshness of fish, we are all pretty good at spotting liars! Then take a serious look at the fish itself. Lift the gill covers and look at the gills (on the head, round about where their ears would be). If the gills are a deep pink or red, and if they look bright – not dull and slimy – that is a good sign. The tail should be well shaped and not ragged. The fish should be bright-eyed. If it's a flat fish the body should be firm – give it a prod with your finger – and it should feel 'heavy', if it feels light and flabby then it may be full of eggs which means you're buying more roe than flesh. Most important of all, use your nose. Fresh fish doesn't smell, not even the guts. You'll notice that even a busy market like this one doesn't smell of fish.

There are some oysters over there. How do you open them at home?

Opening oysters is one of those skills which we would all be master of, if only we got enough practice. At the restaurant we open about two thousand a week, so all the chefs are pretty good. Do not resort to those new-fangled oyster-opening gadgets – there's a thing like a pair of pliers which just crushes the edges of the shells until the oyster surrenders – you simply end up with gritty oysters. For most of us the best oyster-opening gadget is a fishmonger.

What are the main differences between Native Oysters and Rock Oysters?

Technically speaking, Natives are *ostrea edulis* and Rocks are *crassotrea gigas*. Rock oysters are also known as 'Pacific' oysters and do well in warm water – which is why they do not follow the 'only-when-there's-an-R-in-the-month' rule. The Native oyster is Britain's indigenous oyster, slower growing and a lover of cool water. There are less of them and they are more expensive. As to the taste, you have to be a regular and committed oyster eater to tell them apart in a blind tasting, but most people give the crown to Natives … perhaps that's another reason why they are more expensive.

How do you tell a good oyster ?

To start with they need to be firmly shut. When opened they should be wet, with surplus seawater sloshing around; they should be plump and glossy, and they should never smell nasty.

Which do you think is the most underrated fish?

I'd put two kinds of fish in joint first place – pollock and whiting. Admittedly they haven't got a very strong taste, but when fresh they are just the thing to use for fishcakes or faggots. They bind well and have the perfect texture for such dishes. They are also cheap.

I'm a big fan of crab. Which do you think is the better buy, a cock or a hen crab ?

I always pick a hen crab for myself, but that's because I prefer the brown meat, and although the claw – and thus the amount of white meat – is smaller on a hen crab, there's much more yummy brown meat.

How do you tell when a crab is fresh?

At the restaurant we always buy them alive. They should feel heavy and be energetic. If you are buying a crab that has already been cooked, you should look out for one where the brown meat is still shiny and has not gone dull. The 'dead men's fingers' should be fluffy and not bedraggled.

While we are at it, what should you look out for when choosing a lobster?

There are two rules. The first is that you should choose one that is sweet-smelling and has a firm shell. The second is purely about size. If you have the option you should always choose a lobster that is between 1 kg and 2 kg. Any larger than 2 kg and the meat will be tough. Any smaller than 1 kg and not only is the shell-to-meat ratio less favourable, but the meat tends to be watery. When you get a nice lobster weighing between 1 kg and 2 kg, the claws will have grown big enough to contain plenty of meat while the tail has not yet grown so large that it is tough.

I notice that the Livebait menu often stipulates 'line caught' sea bass. How does this make a difference?

They are better fish. It's as simple as that. The ones that come from trawlers get rolled around in the nets and damaged, they also tend to bleed a lot, which spoils the fish. When fish are netted, the change of pressure as they are brought up to the surface can empty their stomachs, which leaves them flabby. You must also remember that trawlers stay out at sea for a lot longer than the smaller boats that fish with lines. Line-caught fish is usually fresher fish, so as well as being better for the environment it makes better eating.

I bet you'd tell me the same story about 'diver caught' scallops?

Getting hold of large, fresh, top-quality scallops is even more of a headache. I like the ones we get from the divers in Scotland. The traditional scallop dredgers just tow a huge beam along the bottom of the sea, which scrapes up every living thing and leaves a featureless mud behind. It may take years for the seabed to regenerate. Divers can literally hand-pick the scallops, leaving the little ones to grow on. Of course, using divers can lead to unforeseen problems especially in the winter when the weather is bad: one week, the divers working for our suppliers were trapped on a remote island in the West of Scotland by a fierce storm. For several days there was no sign of the divers and no sign of any scallops. We had to take them off the menu.

What's the difference between a brill and a turbot, and why do they call some fish chicken turbot?
I don't know why they are called 'chicken', but the term is sometimes used for smaller turbot –
up to about 800 grams. Chicken turbot are good eating, though not a patch on the texture
and flavour of a bigger fish. Turbot is slightly firmer, and has a more pronounced flavour than
brill. You can always tell a turbot because it is usually a lot darker than a brill and is covered
in warts, lumps and spikes.

Two other fish that can often get muddled are Dover and lemon soles. How do you tell them apart?
The Dover sole is a very classy fish, firm and full of flavour. The lemon sole is a definite second best – a poor person's sole. Once filleted, all manner of flat fish, right down to the humble dab, can be passed off by unscrupulous chefs as sole, but while some may look the same, and even taste similar, the texture is what shows them up immediately. Dover sole is so firm it is almost like meat.

Why do you insist on undyed smoked haddock in your recipes?

Don't be silly! When you taste something, are you likely to enjoy it more if it is a bright fluorescent yellow? Dye doesn't make the fish taste any different, and we certainly don't need to ingest any more chemicals than we already do.

You also seem to be a fan of wild salmon. Why's that?

Next time you have the opportunity, compare a wild salmon with his farmed brother. The wild fish will have a clean, streamlined look and a square tail; the farmed fish will have more of a couch potato look about him. This is not surprising – he has spent his lifetime in a cage. Also note the flabby, fatty flesh of the farmed salmon, and the tail and fins, which are often ragged. Wild salmon always eats better, but the salmon-farming industry is aware of these problems and is developing new ways to narrow the gap in quality. One of the most successful initiatives has been to relocate the salmon cages further out to sea in strong tidal currents, which is one way of guaranteeing the growing fish more exercise. So the rule is, wild salmon if you can get it and farmed salmon if you cannot, and the same rule applies when you're buying smoked salmon as well.

What's the most troublesome ingredient you use in the restaurant?

The one that gives us the most headaches is the langoustine. Every day the demand for langoustines outstrips supply, and the UK market is put under even greater pressure by the Spanish, French and Portuguese agents. Prices can soar with just a hint of bad weather. What's more, langoustines are very fragile, our suppliers deliver them alive, in sea water and each in its own rigid plastic tube to stop damage from fighting or accidents. You can tell when they are top quality: the langoustine are lively, and have good hard shells, especially around their heads. They are also the most wonderful eating, we put them on the menu steamed. No frills, just the natural sweetness of the fresh langoustine . . . delicious.

What's the most rewarding thing about cooking fish?

At Livebait we get all sorts of customers. From the fish fanatics, to people who rarely – if ever – choose fish when they are out. For so many Brits, eating fish begins and ends with battered cod and chips, so introducing them to the sweetness of a seared scallop, or the wonderful texture of a piece of roasted brill is terribly exciting. Fish doesn't have to be full of bones; it doesn't have to be an oddity you eat only on Friday; it doesn't even have to be difficult to cook. Fish can be simple and delicious. When you see someone change their mind about fish, that's the most rewarding thing of all.

fish tales

Introduction

Most cookbooks are divided up into sections by ingredients, or by seasons of the year, or by particular courses of a meal. This one isn't. We thought it more helpful to divide the dishes into sections on the basis of who you would cook them for. This works well, if the restaurant is anything to judge by – a pair of young lovers enjoying a romantic date never order the same dishes as a businessman entertaining his bank manager, while at home you would cook different dishes for your family from the ones you could show off with at a grand dinner party.

So 'Starters and Suppers' contains all the recipes that would make good starters in a multi-course meal or informal supper dishes in their own right. 'Family meals' means, well, meals for the family. 'Grandstand dishes' are the ones for boasting about, which will enhance your reputation on the dinner-party circuit. 'Dinners à deux' are recipes for two that err on the romantic and extravagant side. 'Dishes from left field' take their name from the American expression 'coming out of left field', which is a sporting term meaning completely unexpected and surprising. These are dishes that use novel combinations of ingredients or original techniques, they are generally pretty unusual and tend to be daring. 'Breads', 'Sweets', and 'Pickles, preserves and sauces' are all self-explanatory.

It only remains to proffer a touch of clarification,

- *Light olive oil* means standard, everyday, inexpensive olive oil.
- *Good olive oil* means extra-virgin, the good stuff you keep for dressings and drizzling.
- *Eggs* are medium eggs – especially important in the baking recipes.
- *Salt* is sea salt.
- *Pepper* is freshly ground black pepper.
- Generally, the presentation suggested in the 'Shopping and showing off' section for each dish, is tailored to the domestic kitchen. Sometimes at the restaurant, dishes are arranged slightly differently. This is why some of the pictures (which were all taken at Livebait) show a more exotic and fanciful presentation. Rest assured, the dishes will taste just as good however they are plated-up!

Weights and Measures

All recipes are written to metric. They can be converted to imperial by using the following tables. Do not combine metric and imperial.

Liquid Conversions

Metric		Imperial
15 ml	=	$\frac{1}{2}$ fl oz
30 ml	=	1 fl oz
50 ml	=	2 fl oz
100 ml	=	$3\frac{1}{2}$ fl oz
125 ml	=	4 fl oz
150 ml	=	5 fl oz ($\frac{1}{4}$ pint)
200 ml	=	7 fl oz ($\frac{1}{3}$ pint)
250 ml ($\frac{1}{4}$ litre)	=	9 fl oz
300 ml	=	10 fl oz ($\frac{1}{2}$ pint)
350 ml	=	12 fl oz
400 ml	=	14 fl oz
425 ml	=	15 fl oz ($\frac{3}{4}$ pint)
450 ml	=	16 fl oz
500 ml ($\frac{1}{2}$ litre)	=	18 fl oz
600 ml	=	1 pint (20 fl oz)
700 ml	=	$1\frac{1}{4}$ pints
850 ml	=	$1\frac{1}{2}$ pints
1 litre	=	$1\frac{3}{4}$ pints
1.2 litres	=	2 pints
1.5 litres	=	$2\frac{3}{4}$ pints
2 litres	=	$3\frac{1}{2}$ pints
2.5 litres	=	$4\frac{1}{2}$ pints
3 litres	=	$5\frac{1}{4}$ pints

Solid Weight Conversions

Metric		Imperial
15 g	=	$\frac{1}{2}$ oz
25 g	=	1 oz
40 g	=	$1\frac{1}{2}$ oz
50 g	=	$1\frac{3}{4}$ oz
75 g	=	$2\frac{3}{4}$ oz
100 g	=	$3\frac{1}{2}$ oz
125 g	=	$4\frac{1}{2}$ oz
150 g	=	$5\frac{1}{2}$ oz
175 g	=	6 oz
200 g	=	7 oz
225 g	=	8 oz
250 g	=	9 oz
275 g	=	$9\frac{1}{2}$ oz
300 g	=	$10\frac{1}{2}$ oz
325 g	=	$11\frac{1}{2}$ oz
350 g	=	12 oz
400 g	=	14 oz
425 g	=	15 oz
450 g	=	1lb
500 g	=	1lb 2 oz
600 g	=	1lb 5 oz
700 g	=	1lb 9 oz
750 g	=	1lb 10oz
1 kg	=	2lb 4 oz
1.25 kg	=	2lb 12 oz
1.5 kg	=	3lb 5 oz
2 kg	=	4lb 8 oz
2.25 kg	=	5lb
2.5 kg	=	5lb 8 oz
3 kg	=	6lb 8 oz

Oven Temperature Conversions

°C	Gas	°F
110	$\frac{1}{4}$	225
120	$\frac{1}{2}$	250
140	1	275
150	2	300
160	3	325
175	4	350
190	5	375
200	6	400
220	7	425
230	8	450
240	9	475
260	10	500

Standards Liquid

1 teaspoon	=	5 ml
1 dessertspoon	=	10 ml
1 tablespoon	=	15 ml

starters and suppers

Gigandaes plaki

You do need to remember to put the beans in to soak a day or so earlier, but from then on this recipe has few pitfalls. The result is stunning. If you can find the large Greek bean called gigandaes use them, otherwise the dish works as well with the humble butter bean. Serves four of the hungriest.

500 g dried gigandaes

500 ml chicken stock (see page 188)

1 dessertspoon salt

1/2 head celery

200 g carrots

200 g shallots

200 g leeks

4 cloves garlic

300 g tinned plum tomatoes

3 bay leaves

70 ml good olive oil

1 Soak the beans for 24 hours.

2 Cover with cold water and bring up to the boil. Cook for an hour, or until the beans are just soft.

3 Then add the chicken stock and salt.

4 Dice the celery and carrots, finely chop the shallots and leeks, peel and crush the garlic, strain the tomatoes from their juice. Add them all, plus the bay leaves, to the pan with the beans, cover and cook together for 30 minutes.

5 Ten minutes before serving, take the pot off the stove and adjust the seasoning, remove the bay leaves, then stir in the olive oil and leave to wait with the lid on.

Shopping and showing off

You may substitute mild onions for shallots. You can use plain water if you have no chicken stock to hand.

Home-cured mackerel
and scrambled eggs

This dish is delicious served hot as a supper dish – just pile the eggs and mackerel on to toast – but also makes an elegant starter when presented cold, turned out of ramekins on to a plate with a leaf salad. Serves four.

4 courgettes

a little good olive oil

100 g butter

8 eggs

pepper

50 ml double cream

4 fillets Home-cured Mackerel (see page 202)

1 Cut the courgettes into thin strips lengthways. Brush with oil and place under a hot grill for a minute until wilted. Use them to line 4 ramekins – they should be big enough to hold 200 ml.

2 Melt the butter in a thick-bottomed pan. Stir the eggs together with 4 twists of ground black pepper, and add to the butter.

3 Stir over a low heat until the eggs start to set. Just before you are left with a solid rubbery mass, take the pan away from the heat and work in the cream. Allow to cool.

4 Skin and flake the mackerel and stir it into the egg mixture. Beware, if you add the mackerel while the mixture is too hot it will 'cook', which accentuates the fishy taste.

5 Pack this mixture into the ramekins and cool before turning out.

Shopping and showing off

This rich dish benefits from some contrasting flavours on the plate – try a salad made from rocket or radicchio leaves and a little Balsamic Vinaigrette (see page 193).

Brandade mash

with poached egg and pak choi

The brandade will bring out the forward planner in you. It's jolly tasty but you must start at least a day ahead. At Livebait, Brandade Mash does sterling service as a vegetable, but with a poached egg and some greens it makes a great supper. This recipe makes enough mash for four.

250 g salt cod

500 ml semi-skimmed milk

I bay leaf

2 cloves garlic

I large fat red chilli

50 ml olive oil

500 g floury potatoes

juice of I lemon

pepper

4 fresh eggs

a bunch of pak choi

I Rehydrate the cod by putting it in fresh water to soak for 8 hours; then change the water and leave it for another 8 hours; then repeat the procedure a third time. By which time your piece of cod will be considerably bigger.

2 Infuse the milk with the bay leaf by bringing to the boil and leaving to simmer for 20 minutes.

3 Peel and crush the garlic; seed and chop the chillies finely; cook in a frying pan with a little of the oil until they are softened.

4 Add the salt cod to the milk and cook until it flakes easily – about 35–40 minutes. Strain off the milk and reserve.

5 Pick off the skin, remove any bones, and then flake the fish into a bowl.

6 Peel and boil the potatoes without salt. You want them fairly firm – definitely not mushy. Drain and mash.

7 Beat half the warm milk, the olive oil and the lemon juice into the mash.

8 Add the sautéed chilli and garlic, and finally the cod. Mix thoroughly and adjust seasoning, you'll need pepper but probably no more salt.

9 Poach the eggs and wilt the pak choi in boiling water.

Shopping and showing off

You'll find salt cod in some supermarkets and delicatessens, especially those with a Portuguese clientele. Pak choi is a crisp Chinese vegetable, which is increasingly common in supermarkets and always to be found in Chinese shops; spinach is a fine substitute. You can cook the Brandade Mash in advance but it is difficult to reheat without burning – unless you resort to a microwave.

Salade 'Niçoise'

Those pedantic people who argue about the correct ingredients of a classic salade Niçoise would doubtless be very upset by this the Livebait version. No tuna or anchovies, but Bayonne ham and cooking sake . . . ! Try eating it. Whatever it is called makes little difference – it eats very well indeed. Salad for four.

100 g fine green beans

1 artichoke

$\frac{1}{2}$ red pepper

$\frac{1}{2}$ green pepper

60 g Bayonne ham

4 plum tomatoes

1 ripe pear

50 g shallots

4 small heads red Belgian endive

12 black olives, pitted

3 tablespoons snipped chives

1 tablespoon freshly squeezed lemon juice

125 ml good olive oil, plus a little extra

50 ml mirin (sweet cooking sake)

salt

1 Blanch the beans in boiling salted water for 3 minutes, remove, plunge into icy cold water to maintain the colour.

2 Boil the artichoke until it is cooked. Remove the two outer layers of leaves to reveal the central choke of hairy fibres. Cut the choke out with a teaspoon. Slice the heart into strips.

3 Chop the peppers into thin strips.

4 Cut the ham into thin strips, fry until crisp in a minimum amount of olive oil. Dry and cool on kitchen paper.

5 Peel and seed the plum tomatoes, and cut them into strips.

6 Peel and core the pear. Cut into slices lengthways.

7 Peel the shallots and chop them finely.

8 Rinse and trim the endives. Peel off the leaves keeping them whole.

9 Combine the beans, artichoke, peppers, ham, tomatoes, pear, shallots, endives, olives and chives in a salad bowl.

starters and suppers

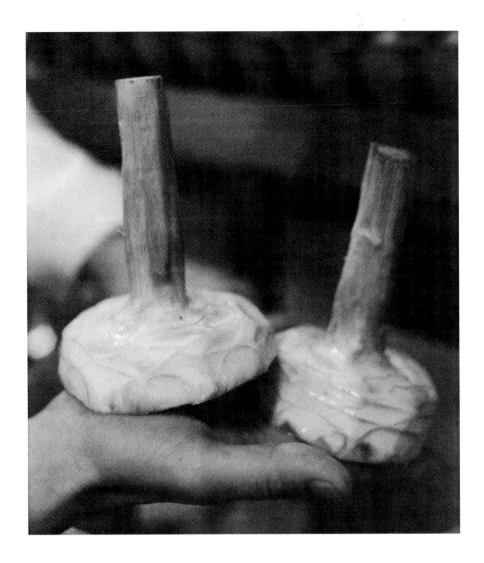

10 Make the dressing in a jug by whisking together the lemon juice, oil and mirin.
Add salt to taste.

11 Toss the salad gently in the dressing and serve.

Shopping and showing off

Pears: if you can find them those large Japanese pears are particularly good, otherwise a large Conference pear is fine. Mirin is a sweet sake specially made for cooking. You'll find it at Japanese grocers and delicatessen shops. Bayonne ham: this very lean ham fries to a crisp and is preferable to pancetta. You need the kind of endive called witloof, or sometimes chicory. Radicchio is *not* suitable. Room temperature: both the tomatoes and the pear will taste better if served at room temperature.

Prawn and mussel sauerkraut

At Livebait, this unlikely-sounding concoction is served as an accompaniment. But when you taste it you will discover that it is good enough to stand alone. Seriously delicious, and very simple. Serves four.

200 g sauerkraut

50 g unsalted butter

300 g mussels – meat only

150 ml dry white wine

150 g large, peeled, cooked prawns

a bunch of dill leaves (1 × 15 g supermarket pack)

1 Rinse the sauerkraut in a colander under the tap. Cut the butter into cubes and put it into the refrigerator to chill.

2 If you are using fresh mussels, open them by shaking them in a pan over a low flame. Pick them over, discarding any that have not opened, shell the rest and reserve the meat.

4 Heat the sauerkraut through in a non-reactive pan with the wine.

5 When it is hot add the prawns and mussels and allow them to heat through.

6 Strain off the liquid into another pan to finish the sauce. Put the lid back on, and keep the sauerkraut warm.

7 Bring the juices to the boil. Take the cold butter and whisk it into the boiling sauce so that it thickens and becomes glossy.

8 Take the pan off the heat and stir the sauce back into the sauerkraut. Snip the dill into the mixture and stir in. Heat through and serve immediately.

Shopping and showing off

Sauerkraut comes in large jars or tins and is available in most supermarkets, experiment to find which brand is least salty. The mussels can be either live or frozen – as a rough guide, 450 g of frozen is the equivalent of just under 300 g when thawed. Prawns that are 'shell on' are often better value as you are not paying high prices for a water glaze covering which you get on frozen ones. It is important not to overcook the mussels and prawns as they will become rubbery if you do. This dish makes an original accompaniment to all kinds of plainly cooked fish.

Chickpea, red wine and black pudding stew

You shouldn't let the requirement for forward planning put you off trying this heart-warming stew, which is loosely based on the Iberian dish Cocido. Start 24 hours in advance. Serves four hungry people.

500 g dried chickpeas
1 litre chicken stock
200 g carrots
300 g peeled shallots
3 stalks celery
4 cloves garlic
1 bay leaf
350 ml red wine – not your best!
400 g black pudding
salt and pepper
25 ml light olive oil

1 Soak the chickpeas in water for 24 hours.

2 Strain the chickpeas, rinse them in fresh water and put them in a pot with the chicken stock. Bring to the boil, turn down the heat, cover the pan and simmer for 45 minutes.

3 Dice the vegetables, peel and slice the garlic, and add to the pot with the wine and bay leaf. Simmer for 30 minutes more.

4 Take 100 g of the black pudding, skin it, chop it up, and stir into the stew to thicken the juices: adjust the seasoning to taste.

5 Cut the remaining black pudding into slices on the bias (i.e. diagonally, across) and cook quickly in a hot frying pan with a little oil to crisp up the outside.

6 Ladle the stew into a soup bowl and top with some of the fried black pudding.

Shopping and showing off

How to choose a black pudding is a very personal matter: they range all the way from highly perfumed, large bore, commercially made puddings, to smaller, harder ring sausages handmade by butchers. Small-diameter puddings seem to fry crisper.

Lime polenta fries with mayonnaise

A dish to upset every living Belgian! Crisp on the outside and soft inside, these fries work well with any mayonnaise from the luxurious and home made to the bottled and shop bought.

2 fleshy red chillies

10 spring onions

1 bunch coriander (1 × 15 g supermarket pack)

750 ml water

salt and pepper

300 g instant polenta

zest and juice of 4 limes

75 ml olive oil

oil for deep frying

mayonnaise

1 Seed and chop the chillies very finely. Chop the spring onions, and the coriander. Put them to one side.

2 Bring the water to the boil and add 1 tablespoon of salt.

3 Add the polenta and stir continually while it thickens into a porridge.

4 Lower the heat and add the lime zest and juice, the chillies, the spring onions, the coriander and the olive oil. Keep stirring until well mixed. Adjust the seasoning with salt and pepper – it may need salt.

5 Pour into a large tray, (so that the polenta is no deeper than 2 cm) and place in the refrigerator.

6 When completely cold and set, cut into large chip shapes (7 cm × 2 cm × 2 cm deep).

7 Roll the chips in flour and deep fry in hot oil (preferably in olive oil) for 4–5 minutes, until crisp and cooked.

Shopping and showing off

This is a simple dish which you can vary to suit your tastes: experiment with different flavourings. Shop bought mayonnaise is fine, simple is best.

Salmon and dill ravioli

If you can get fresh ravioli pasta from a helpful Italian delicatessen, do so – but you will miss out on the fun of making your own. Makes sixteen generous ravioli.

300 g raw salmon

100 ml crème fraîche *or* sour cream

1 bunch fresh dill (1 × 15 g supermarket pack)

salt and pepper

1 teaspoon fresh paprika

1 quantity Simple Pasta Dough (see page 200)

1 Skin and bone the salmon, chop it into small dice, and put it in a bowl. Add the crème fraîche. Snip the dill and stir it all together. Season well – salt, pepper and the paprika.

2 Roll out the dough as thin as possible. Then cut out pairs of circles about 10 cm across. Put a good dollop of the mixture in the centre of each one and superimpose the lid. Use your fingers to crimp the edges shut. Be firm!

3 Poach in salty boiling water to which a tiny bit of olive oil has been added. The ravioli will only take 7–8 minutes, or maybe a little longer depending on the thickness of the pasta. Do no more than 3 at a time unless you have a very big pan. Keep warm until you serve.

Shopping and showing off

For a starter serve 3 of these ravioli with a dribble of melted butter and some green leaves. As a supper dish, try 4 with a dipping sauce – a puddle of the simple Pernod Sauce goes well (see page 194).

Smoked haddock and cockle quiche

You can substitute octopus for cockles in this simple but delicious dish. Then it becomes the perfect way to use up any spare partly cooked octopus you may have left over after making recipes like the one on page 114 for Honey and ginger roast octopus. Serves four as a generous starter.

300 g shop-bought shortcrust pastry

25 g butter

75 g leeks

75 g shallots

75 g carrots

1 tablespoon light olive oil

125 g undyed smoked haddock

125 g shelled cockles

3 eggs

75 ml crème fraîche

75 ml double cream

½ bunch tarragon (½ × 15g supermarket packet)

25 g caperberries

salt and pepper to taste

1 Preheat your oven to 230°C/450°F/gas mark 8.

2 Butter a deep flan tin – 20–22 cm in diameter by 3 cm deep.

3 Roll out the shortcrust pastry and line the tin. Prick the base with a fork. Butter a piece of foil and line the inside of the pastry case fitting it closely to the sides. Fill with beans and bake blind for 7–8 minutes until the pastry is set but only just.

4 Remove the liner and prick the base again, press the sides up if they have started to slip down. Replace the liner and beans and cook on for another 5 minutes. Now the pastry should be cooked but not coloured.

5 Remove the liner and bake for a further 2–3 minutes until the pastry is nicely coloured. Let the oven cool down to 190°C/375°F/gas mark 5.

6 Allow the pastry to cool in the tin and then take it out ... very carefully.

7 Meanwhile, peel and chop the leeks, shallots and carrots and cook in olive oil until softened.

8 Skin the haddock and cut it into chunks. Rinse the cockles.

9 Beat together the eggs, crème fraîche, and double cream. Strip the tarragon leaves from the stalks, chop them roughly and add them. Add the caperberries. Season the mixture – be careful with the salt but it may need some.

10 Put a sheet of baking parchment on to a baking sheet and stand the flan case on it. Put the mixed fish and vegetables in, and then add the egg mixture so that it is filled to within 5 mm of the rim. Bake for 30 minutes.

Shopping and showing off

Following this method you can make the quiche base a day ahead and fill and cook it only when required. If you can find fresh cockles so much the better, if not frozen or pickled ones will suffice (454 g of frozen cockles yields about 290 g when thawed). This quiche begs to be served with a small salad – a few mixed leaves, preferably undressed, otherwise the dressing would fight with the flavours of the quiche. You can serve the quiche hot or cold, but if cold, try and make it more like 'room temperature', lukewarm; the flavours will be much improved.

37

Potato and hazelnut gratin

This makes a splendid supper dish with the addition of a few rashers of well-crisped streaky bacon to give a contrasting texture. It also makes a great support act: try it with the Whole Stuffed Black Bream (see page 92). Serves four.

150 g hazelnuts, unblanched

200 ml double cream

salt, pepper and nutmeg

1 kg potatoes

25 g warm butter

2 cloves garlic

1 Preheat your oven to 220°C/425°F/gas mark 7.

2 Prepare the hazelnuts by roasting them for 4–5 minutes on a tray in the very hot oven. Remove – turn the oven down to 150°C/300°F/gas mark 2 – and as they cool, rub off the skins with your fingers. Crush them with a pestle and mortar, or by folding them in a tea towel and rolling a bottle over them. Your objective is small chunky pieces not dust.

3 Bring the cream to the boil, season with salt and pepper, and some grated nutmeg.

4 Peel and then slice the potatoes paper thin, using a mandolin, rinse in cold water to get rid of excess starch, then add them to the cream.

5 Use half the butter to grease a large gratin dish – pick one big enough (it is important that your finished layer of potato mixture is no more than 2 cm thick) or prepare 4 individual ramekins. Crush the garlic and spread over the bottom of the dish or dishes.

6 Lift out the potato slices with a slotted spoon and arrange two or three layers of them in the dish; then dribble on a layer of cream; then a layer of hazelnuts; then cream; then potatoes; then cream; then potatoes; then hazelnuts.

7 Cover with foil and bake for 60 minutes for a large gratin and 30 minutes for ramekins. Check whether the potato is cooked by testing with a knife through the foil. Then remove the foil and allow to brown. If necessary brown the top still further under the grill before serving.

Egg tagliatelle

with mussels and Merguez sausage

This is another Livebait 'surprise package'. It started life playing a supporting role in the Tiger Prawn and Sea Bass dish on page 94, but as more and more customers sang its praises it became obvious that it had claims to be a dish in its own right. Serves four as a generous starter, or three as a supper.

1 kg mussels

1 red onion

1 clove of garlic

1 fat red chilli

50 ml olive oil

200 g Merguez sausage

500 g fresh *or* dried egg tagliatelle

salt

2 eggs

150 ml double cream

$\frac{1}{2}$ bunch fresh parsley ($\frac{1}{2} \times$ 15g supermarket pack)

pepper

1 Steam the mussels until they open, and pick out the meat, discard any that remain closed.

2 Finely chop the onion, crush the garlic, seed and chop the chilli – then cook them in a large frying pan with a little of the olive oil, until they soften.

3 While this is happening, prick the Merguez sausages with a fork to stop them bursting and blanch them for 3–4 minutes in a large pan of boiling water, take out with a slotted spoon and cut into 50-mm slices.

4 Bring the Merguez water back to the boil, and add a dessertspoon of salt, 10 ml of olive oil and the tagliatelle. Cook for 2–3 minutes; the pasta should be perceptibly undercooked. Strain off the water.

5 Beat together the egg and cream in a bowl with the snipped parsley leaves. Reserve.

6 Add the Merguez slices to the onion mixture in the frying pan and make sure they are cooked through. Add the mussels and the remaining olive oil. Stir the mixture. Add the pasta, and pour over the egg and cream; mix thoroughly over a low heat until everything is warmed through. Adjust seasoning and serve immediately.

French beans tarator

At Livebait this is one of the more straightforward vegetable accompaniments on offer – crunchy French beans with a rich walnut sauce. It's so good, that it makes a splendid starter, and if you feel adventurous and spendthrift you could always substitute **Brazil nuts for** the walnuts – it will at least save you the chore of skinning the walnuts. Serves four as a starter or six in its role as an accompanying vegetable.

4 slices of your favourite white bread

150 ml good olive oil

180 g skinned walnuts *or* Brazil nuts

2 cloves garlic

100 ml balsamic vinegar

salt, pepper and sweet paprika to taste

500 g extra fine French beans

1 Cut the crusts from the bread and soften the crumb in a little water, then squeeze it dry by hand. Put it in a food processor (or liquidiser) and, with the motor on slow, gradually add the oil, then the nuts (if you're using Brazils it is sensible to pre-chop them a bit with a heavy knife), peeled garlic cloves and the vinegar. When you have a sauce with a smooth, creamy consistency adjust the seasoning with salt, pepper and sweet paprika.

2 Top and tail the beans, and then blanch them in boiling salted water for 3–4 minutes.

3 Put the sauce and the beans into a dry pan and warm through, do not get too hot or the sauce will split.

Shopping and showing off

At Livebait we make the Tarator Sauce using Sun-dried Tomato Bread (see page 153) but any good, firm bread will do. The more character the bread has the better, but very dense wholemeal breads do not absorb so much oil, and you may have to drizzle some extra on to the plate to lubricate the dish.

Goat's cheese cheesecake

This makes a good starter (experiment with individual parcels) or a great family supper dish as a single large cheesecake. Serves four.

2 × 30 cm × 30 cm sheets from a packet of filo pastry

50 g butter, melted

3 tablespoons Onion Jam (see page 182)

100 g grated Parmesan

100 g curd goat's cheese *or* any soft, mild goat's cheese

75 ml crème fraîche

2 eggs

1 teaspoon paprika

salt and pepper

1 quantity tomato chutney (see page 180)

1 Preheat your oven to 160°C/325°F/gas mark 3.

2 Line a 20-cm loose-bottomed flan tin with 2 layers of filo pastry, brushing the first with butter before adding the second. Leave as much filo as possible overhanging the edge.

3 Use a food processor or liquidiser to whoosh the Onion Jam, Parmesan, goat's cheese, crème fraîche and eggs. Season with the paprika, and salt and pepper to taste.

4 Pour the mixture into the centre of the filo and fold in the ears. Brush the top with melted butter.

5 Bake for 2–3 hours. Start testing after two hours. The cake is done when a knife driven into the centre and withdrawn feels hot on the lips.

Shopping and showing off

Curd goat's cheese will give you the best possible combination of taste and texture: ask at a specialist cheese shop or the supermarket cheese counter. You can serve this cheesecake with a good dollop of tomato chutney.

Smoked haddock,
leek and potato broth with a quail's egg

This is a rich broth containing good-sized chunks of haddock and finished with a quail's egg that is allowed to poach in the bowl of boiling soup on the way to the table. The recipe will serve four as a starter or make a good supper for two.

1 kg plum tomatoes

salt and pepper

1 bunch basil (1 × supermarket plant in pot)

$\frac{1}{2}$ bunch parsley ($\frac{1}{2}$ × 15 g supermarket pack)

$\frac{1}{2}$ bunch thyme ($\frac{1}{2}$ × 15 g supermarket pack)

250 g leeks

250 g waxy potatoes (like Charlotte)

500 g undyed smoked haddock fillet

1 litre chicken stock (see page 188) or vegetable stock (see page 189)

$\frac{1}{2}$ teaspoon smoked hot paprika

4 quail's eggs

I Preheat your oven to 130°C/250°F/gas mark $\frac{1}{2}$ – it shouldn't take long!

2 Cut the tomatoes in half lengthways and arrange them on a baking sheet, sprinkle with sea salt and pepper, and half of the basil, parsley and thyme. Bake in the oven for 2 hours until they are wrinkled and dry-looking. Allow to cool, and purée them in a food processor.

3 Wash the leeks and cut into 2-cm lengths. Peel and dice the potatoes.

4 Skin the haddock fillets and chop them into large bite-sized pieces.

5 Bring the stock to the boil in a large pot. Add the tomato purée and stir until amalgamated. Reduce the heat and simmer for 10 minutes.

6 Add the leeks and potatoes and simmer for a further 25 minutes until the potatoes are cooked but still firm.

7 Add the remaining herbs, the smoked paprika, and the pieces of haddock, simmer for a further 5 minutes. Adjust the seasoning with salt and pepper.

Shopping and showing off

The yellow, dyed, smoked haddock makes an adequate substitute for the unsmoked kind, but why should you consume more chemicals than you have to? Yellow fish doesn't look better or taste better. If you cannot find the smoked red paprika picante, ordinary paprika will do – although it is not as tasty. If you use the vegetable stock option this becomes a good dish for non meat-eaters. To serve, pour the boiling broth into the bowls, be sure that the bits of fish are evenly distributed, and crack a quail's egg into the centre of the soup. The heat will poach the tiny egg on the way to the table.

family
meals

Halibut parcels in Cos lettuce, with avgolemono sauce and baby vegetables (*see opposite*) 48   Smoked haddock, potato and parsnip rösti, sautéed spinach and a poached egg 50   **Pan-fried turmeric grey mullet with Middle Eastern rice and cumin sauce 52**   Steamed fillet of sole with lentils 54   **Devilled herrings with roast beetroot and turmeric potatoes 56**   Hotpot of cod cheeks, globe artichokes and button mushrooms with potato bread and aïoli 58   **Grilled red mullet with gigandaes plaki and tapenade 61**   Roast cod with couscous crust served with a chickpea, red wine and black pudding stew 62   **Grilled polenta cake, roast tomatoes and tsatsiki 64**   John Dory, spinach and potato pie with Pernod sauce 66   **Tuna with honey-roast chicken wings and lentil stew 69**   Seared scallops with red wine pears 70   **Fisherman's soup 75**   Seared salmon with potato, coriander and lemon-grass Dauphinoise, and an artichoke dressing 77   **Grilled smoked sturgeon with 'nero' spinach and paprika sour cream 78**   Roast monkfish tail with braised red cabbage 80

Halibut parcels in Cos lettuce,
with avgolemono sauce and baby vegetables

The sauce that smothers these halibut parcels and baby vegetables is derived from the famous Greek soup made from eggs and lemons – a combination of ingredients that at first glance seem to have 'curdle' written all over them. Follow the simple steps and you'll end up with an interesting frothy sauce that is both rich and tangy – perfect with the sweet fish and young vegetables. Serves four.

16 outside leaves from 2 large Cos lettuces

300 g raw prawns

8 thin *or* 4 fat spring onions

1 tablespoon sweet paprika

8 chunks halibut, weighing about 50 g each

12 baby carrots

12 baby fennel

12 baby leeks

12 shallots

500 ml chicken stock (see page 188)

150 ml white wine

1 tablespoon cornflour

3 eggs, separated

juice of 2 small lemons *or* 1 large

salt and pepper

1 Wilt the lettuce leaves in boiling water and refresh them in cold water, this will make them manageable.

2 Shell the prawns, and remove the black veins which run down their backs, mince them or chop them very finely. Chop the spring onions finely. Mix with the prawns.

3 Spread the mixture on to the lettuce leaves, place a bit of halibut on top of each, dust with paprika, then more prawn, then roll up into neat parcels. If necessary, use two leaves per parcel to make a water-tight envelope. Put to one side.

4 Peel and trim as necessary and then put the baby carrots, fennel, leeks and shallots into the bottom of a large pot and add the chicken stock and wine. Bring to the boil, then simmer for 20 minutes.

5 Carefully place the fish parcels on top of the vegetables and cook with the lid on for another 8–10 minutes, no more, depending on the thickness of your parcels.

6 Gently tip all the liquid from the pot into another pan to finish the sauce, holding back the vegetables and fish with the lid.

7 Slake the cornflour in a little cold water and whisk into the liquid.

8 Simmer until thickened, then turn off the heat.

9 Whisk the egg whites in a bowl until they peak, then fold in the yolks.

10 Pour the warm stock into the egg mixture, stirring with a whisk. Put the bowl over a saucepan of boiling water and gradually whisk in the lemon juice. Continue to whisk until the sauce thickens like custard. Adjust seasoning with salt and pepper.

11 Return the sauce to the pot of fish parcels and vegetables, leave for 5 minutes to amalgamate the flavours before serving.

Shopping and showing off

Either medallions of a large halibut or fillets from a small 'chicken' halibut work well with this dish. Baby vegetables are widely available in supermarkets, but if you cannot find any, substitute uniformly sized batons cut from ordinary vegetables. Serve in a soup bowl.

Smoked haddock, potato and parsnip rösti, sautéed spinach and a poached egg

The strength of this dish lies in the array of textures it provides. There's the fish, the crisp rösti, the spinach ... and just when you think it's all sounding a bit too dry there's the poached egg yolk. Delightful. Serves six.

500 g large potatoes

500 g parsnips

2 bunches spring onions

1 bunch chervil (1 × 15 g supermarket pack)

salt and black pepper

110 ml good olive oil

6 × 125 g undyed smoked haddock fillets

1 garlic clove

50 g butter

500 g washed spinach

4 eggs

500 ml water

100 ml white wine vinegar

1 Preheat your oven, and a flat baking sheet to 220°C/425°F/gas mark 7.

2 Peel the potatoes and parsnips, and grate them into a large bowl. Chop the spring onions and the chervil and add them. Season with salt and pepper. Mix thoroughly, adding 50 ml of the olive oil.

3 Cook the rösti in two batches. Heat a large frying pan with 25 ml of the oil in it. Press half the rösti mixture into the hot pan in a flat layer.

4 Cook on a moderately high heat until the bottom crisps up. Then turn it over on to the hot baking sheet. Repeat with the second lot of mixture.

5 Oil the haddock fillets and put them on to another baking sheet.

6 Put both the sheets into the oven for 10 minutes (the rösti gets the hottest part of your oven – probably the top). Check the rösti after 5 minutes.

7 In the meantime, crush the garlic. Put the remaining 10 ml of oil in a large pan, and cook the garlic until it begins to soften. Add the spinach, stir until it has wilted completely. Press out the liquid that has formed while cooking, season and keep warm.

8 Poach the eggs in the water and vinegar. You are aiming for a runny yolk. Skin the haddock.

Shopping and showing off

To serve, cut a wedge from the rösti – or punch out a small circular rösti using a pastry-cutter – and crown it with the spinach, haddock and, finally, the poached egg. Part of the fun of this 'tall food' is the joy of being a vandal as you push it over with your knife and fork.

Pan-fried turmeric grey mullet
with Middle Eastern rice and cumin sauce

Grey mullet is a meaty and much underrated fish. Make sure your fishmonger fillets it carefully for you and the bigger the fish he starts with the better. If possible always choose mullet caught on the open sea (at Livebait, we get some splendid ones from Guernsey). Estuarine fish can taste 'muddy'. The accompanying rice dish is straight from the spice markets and deliciously squelchy. Accompany it with the Cumin Sauce.

1 teaspoon cumin seeds

1 teaspoon coriander seeds

250 g Spanish onions

250 g leeks

a little olive oil

1 kg leaf spinach

1 bunch basil (1 × 15g supermarket plant in a pot)

100 g long grain rice – 'easy-cook'

1 teaspoon ground cinnamon

2 × tablespoons ground turmeric

100 g sultanas

juice of 1 lemon

40 ml good olive oil

salt and pepper

50 g plain flour

1 tablespoon salt

4 grey mullet fillets each weighing approximately 150 g

30 ml olive oil

1 quantity Cumin Sauce (see page 197)

1 To prepare the rice. In a dry frying pan toast the cumin and coriander seeds; crush them, using a pestle and mortar, or a grinder.

2 Chop the onions and leeks finely and cook in a large saucepan with a little oil until they have softened. Add the cumin and coriander.

3 Wash the spinach, remove the stalks, and tear it up roughly by hand. Tear up the basil. Add them both to the saucepan, then turn down the heat as low as possible, and put the lid on for a minute or two until the spinach is soft.

4 Add the rice with 200 ml of water, the cinnamon and a tablespoon of turmeric. Put the lid back on and cook slowly for 30 minutes, stirring occasionally and adding more water if the contents get dry.

5 The rice should be quite sloppy. When it's cooked add the sultanas and the lemon juice and stir well. Then stir in 40 ml good olive oil and leave to stand off the heat with the lid on. Adjust seasoning.

6 Mix the flour, a tablespoon of turmeric and salt and use it to coat the mullet fillets.

7 Fry in a little hot olive oil. They will be done after about 3 minutes a side.

Shopping and showing off

Grey mullet is one of those fish that needs to be very fresh. If you cannot find grey mullet with a sparkle in their eyes, change the plan and use a nice Dover sole. To serve, make an island of rice in the centre of the plate – use a pastry ring or mould to make the rice 'island' perfectly regular – then top with a fillet of fish, and surround with the Cumin Sauce (see page 197).

Steamed fillet of sole with lentils

As Theodore's mother would say, 'This is a Sunday dish.' Rich and earthy, a combination of flavours that works well together. A genuinely unfussy dish, which may not look elegant on the plate but which certainly stars in the taste department. Serves four.

1 quantity Lentil Stew (see page 201)

250 g fennel

1 orange

75 ml crème fraîche

4 sole fillets

salt and pepper

a little butter

balsamic vinegar

good olive oil

1 Prepare the lentil stew in advance using the recipe on page 201. It will keep for up to a day.
2 Chop the fennel very finely; peel and take all the pith off the orange segments before chopping them roughly. Mix them, and the fennel, into the crème fraîche .
3 Season each sole fillet with salt and pepper, and then roll it up like a Swiss roll using a quarter of the crème fraîche mixture as 'jam'.
4 Wrap each fillet in buttered foil and stab a few holes in the parcel. Steam until cooked – about 10–15 minutes. The parcel will be firm when pressed.

Shopping and showing off

Get your fishmonger to fillet a large sole – Dover for preference, but you can substitute lemon sole. Try to get a large fish – around 650 g – that way a single fillet makes a fine portion. If you cannot find such a fish you may have to buy two and double up. To present the dish, unwrap the sole – any buttery juices can be added to the lentils – and arrange a mound of lentils on each plate. Then drizzle over some balsamic vinegar (cider vinegar would make an acceptable substitute) and a little good olive oil. If you are using a large fish, cut each fillet in half to give two 'roulade' slices. Arrange these on the lentils on each plate.

Devilled herrings
with roast beetroot and turmeric potatoes

The herring is a rich and oily fish, well able to look after itself in the company of these powerful flavours. The tradition of 'devilling' fish and meats is an old and honourable one, although the Livebait style leans more to North Africa than to the gentlemen's clubs of St James's. Serves four.

3 teaspoons cumin seeds

2 teaspoons cayenne pepper

2 teaspoons sea salt

75 ml light olive oil

2 eggs

8 large herring fillets

3 medium raw beetroots

1 tablespoon honey

2 bay leaves

500 g new potatoes

1 teaspoon turmeric

1 fat red chilli

2 garlic cloves

½ bunch fresh coriander (½ × 15 g supermarket pack)

80 g crisp breadcrumbs

4 tablespoons Greek yoghurt

1 Preheat your oven to 200°C/400°F/gas mark 6.

2 Prepare the devilling mix for the herrings. Take a pestle and mortar and grind up the cumin seeds with the cayenne and a teaspoon of the salt. Make into a paste with a dessertspoon of the olive oil. Beat this mixture into the eggs.

3 Marinate the herring fillets in the spicy egg wash while you prepare the vegetables.

4 Put the beetroot into a roasting tray with 200 ml of water, the honey and the bay leaves. Roast for about 60 minutes.

5 Wash, but do not peel, the new potatoes. Then dice them. Put 40 ml of the olive oil into a frying pan and get it hot, then fry the potatoes until tender and crispy. Then add the turmeric, and the remaining teaspoon of salt. Seed the chilli, chop finely and add to the pan. Peel and crush the garlic cloves then add them. Cook on for 2–3 minutes.

6 Finally, add the leaves from the coriander chopped roughly. When they have wilted in the heat the potatoes are ready.

7 Roll the marinated herrings in the breadcrumbs and then pan fry them in the remaining 25 ml of olive oil until golden, turning once – for about 3 minutes a side, less if the fillets are small.

Shopping and showing off

Ask your fishmonger to fillet the herrings for you, and do try to get large ones as they have a better texture when cooked. To assemble the dish on the plate, start with a spoonful of the turmeric potatoes, then peel and slice the beetroot and arrange on top. Finally add 2 herring fillets per person and a tablespoon of thick Greek yoghurt.

Hotpot of cod cheeks,
globe artichokes and button mushrooms
with potato bread and aïoli

This is a rich dish, and provides one occasion when you should certainly consider partnering fish with red wine. The only pricy ingredients are the artichoke hearts, and they more than earn their keep. Serves four.

4 globe artichokes

I lemon

2 garlic cloves

170 g button mushrooms

170 g leeks

170 g shallots

2 fat red chillies

½ bunch basil (½ × supermarket plant in a pot)

50 ml olive oil

200 ml white wine

200 ml water

hearts of 2 heads frisée (curly endive)

about 400 g fish (see Shopping and showing off)

salt and pepper

I quantity Aïoli (see page 190)

a loaf of Potato Bread (see page 155)

1 Prepare the artichokes. Take off two layers of leaves and then slice through horizontally. Trim back to reveal the hairy choke in the centre and remove it with a teaspoon. Rub each trimmed heart with a lemon and keep in water, to which a squeeze of lemon has been added to stop it going dark.

2 Peel and crush the garlic, chop the mushrooms, slice the leeks; peel the shallots (but leave them whole), chop and seed the chillies, tear up the basil leaves. Add them all, with the artichokes, to 2 tablespoons of the oil in the bottom of a heavy casserole and cook until everything has taken on a good colour.

3 Add the wine and water.

4 Trim back the curly endives until you are left with the hearts. Add them to the pot, put the lid on and continue to cook on a low heat, until the artichoke hearts are done (they should be soft – like potatoes ready for mashing).

5 Place the rest of the oil in a frying pan and add the fish pieces to firm them up.

6 Use a slotted spoon to transfer the cod cheeks to the pot. Add them to the vegetables and put the lid on. Take off the heat immediately and leave to stand for 10 minutes.

Shopping and showing off

In practice, cod cheeks are those medallions of meat left to the rear of the head when the fillets have been taken off, and they are becoming increasingly hard to find as fishmongers give way to freezer cabinets and fishmongery itself becomes a dying art. For this recipe you need 12 small lumps of firm fish. The meat round a cod's gills, or skate knobs, or even chunks of monkfish all work well. To present on the plate, take an artichoke heart from the pot and use it as a base, top with a spoonful of the Aïoli and pile a few ladlefuls of the hot pot on top. Serve with a slice of toasted Potato Bread or, failing that, a thick slice of good wholemeal.

Grilled red mullet

with gigandaes plaki and tapenade

This dish miraculously seems to add up to more than the sum of its parts. The red mullet is simply treated but remains wonderfully firm and meaty, Gigandaes Plaki, a splendid bean dish, is very traditional – at least in Greece – and the Tapenade offers an additional strong flavour.

4 fillets red mullet, each weighing 150 g

a little light olive oil

sea salt

1 quantity Gigandaes Plaki (see page 24)

a quantity of Tapenade (see page 184)

1 Brush the fillets with a little olive oil and sprinkle with sea salt for seasoning and some crunch.

2 Cook under a hot grill until the fish is firm – about 3 minutes a side, skin side first. When pressed, accurately cooked fish should feel solid and springy rather than yielding.

Shopping and showing off

The most difficult thing about this dish is getting your hands on the right kind of red mullet. At Livebait we put this dish on the menu only when there are large red mullet available. These provide the right kind of substantial meaty fillet – the little fish known as 'rougets' won't really do. If you cannot find the right red mullet, substitute grey mullet fillets, or even monkfish fillets – although more delicately flavoured fish may be swamped by the Gigandaes Plaki and Tapenade combo. Serve in soup bowls or deep plates, a sea of beans with a fish fillet on top, crowned with a spoonful of Tapenade.

Roast cod with couscous crust

served with a chickpea, red wine and black pudding stew

The combination of the fresh-tasting, firm and flaky cod with the rich and earthy chickpea stew is a winner. Serves four.

125 g couscous

juice of 1 orange

25 ml good olive oil

4 × 200 g cod fillets, cut from the thick end

1 quantity Chickpea, Red Wine and Black Pudding Stew (see page 32)

1 Half cook the couscous in boiling water – this will take about 10 minutes – and drain.

2 Preheat your oven to 200°C/400°F/gas mark 6.

3 Warm the orange juice in a non-reactive saucepan, add the couscous and the oil, stir, cover the pot with clingfilm and put to one side in a warm place for an hour or more.

4 Place the cod pieces, skin side down, on a greased baking sheet, brush with a little oil and season well with salt and pepper. Add a thick – 1.5 cm – crust of couscous. Cook in the oven for 8–10 minutes. If you like a particularly crispy crust, finish under a hot grill until browned.

Shopping and showing off

You can use the 'pre-soaked ' couscous available from the supermarkets, if so omit the initial par-boiling stage. Thick cod is best for this dish, which benefits from simple presentation – a soup bowl full of stew topped with a piece of fish.

Grilled polenta cake,

roast tomatoes and tsatsiki

The polenta cake and the roast tomatoes can be prepared the day before, then finished off when you require them. This is both filling and delicious. Serves six hungry people or eight as a starter.

30 g dried porcini mushrooms

30 ml dry white vermouth

6 plum tomatoes

salt and pepper

1 tablespoon dried thyme

3 garlic cloves

75 ml good olive oil

1 cucumber

200 g Greek yoghurt

30 g carrots

30 g fennel bulb

250 ml medium dry wine

1 litre water

500 g instant polenta

12 large cooked prawns

50 g Parma ham

60 g picked mussels

50 g Parmesan

1 Preheat your oven to 110°C/210°F/gas mark ¼.

2 Put the porcini mushrooms to soak in the vermouth.

3 Slice the tomatoes in half, arrange them on a baking sheet and sprinkle with sea salt, and thyme. Peel 2 of the garlic cloves and cut each into 6 slices. Put a slice on top of each tomato half. Drizzle with a tablespoon of olive oil. Put into the oven for an hour.

4 Remove and turn over each tomato with a palette knife. Return to the oven for another hour.

5 Make the Tsatsiki. Peel and seed the cucumber, then dice it very finely. Crush the remaining garlic finely. Add both to the yoghurt. Stir in a tablespoon of the olive oil and season with salt and pepper. Put to one side while the flavours amalgamate.

6 Peel, then chop the carrots finely. Chop the fennel finely. Cook them slowly with the lid on in the wine with 2 tablespoons of the olive oil, and a seasoning of salt and pepper. They should cook for 30 minutes.

7 Add the porcini and any vermouth that hasn't been soaked up. Cook for a further 30 minutes still leaving the lid on.

8 Bring the water to the boil with 1 tablespoon of salt. Add the polenta and stir it continuously as it thickens up and becomes a smooth porridge.

9 Chop the prawns roughly, and chop the Parma ham. Add them and the mussels, the braised vegetables, the Parmesan, and the remaining olive oil to the mixture stirring continually.

10 Take it off the heat, and when all is evenly mixed, pour it into a tray. The polenta should be no more than 2 cm deep. Put the tray into the refrigerator to cool and solidify.

11 When ready to serve, cut the polenta cake into portions 8 cm × 8 cm square and crisp the top under a grill.

Shopping and showing off

Use the polenta cake as a foundation for 2 tomato halves and a dollop of tsatsiki. Always be careful with leftover tsatsiki: a chemical reaction means that the longer you leave it the more acrid the garlic flavour becomes.

John Dory, spinach and potato pie
with Pernod sauce

This pie makes a fine family dish – serve it with mashed potato. At Livebait, a debate continues over whether this pie goes best with the Pernod Sauce (see page 194) or with another sauce – try the Cumin Sauce (see page 197). Serves four.

1 red pepper

1 yellow pepper

200 g spinach

200 g potatoes

500 ml chicken stock

200 g leeks

25 ml olive oil

2 eggs

60 ml double cream

a bunch of fresh tarragon (1 x 15 g supermarket pack)

500 g John Dory fillets

100 g flour

8 sheets from a pack of filo pastry

50 g melted butter

salt and pepper

1 quantity Pernod Sauce (see page 194)

1 Preheat your oven to 220°C/425 °F/gas mark 7.

2 Cut in half and seed the peppers, then roast them briefly (5 minutes) in the oven . Remove and place in a sealed plastic bag. Rub off their skins when cool and wash under the tap. Cut into wide strips. Turn the oven down to 170°C/338°F/gas mark $3\frac{1}{2}$.

3 Wilt the spinach in boiling water, strain and reserve.

4 Peel the potatoes, then slice them very thinly, preferably on a mandolin. Heat the chicken stock in a pan and blanch the potatoes for 8–10 minutes, adding them a few at a time so that they do not clump together. Strain and reserve.

5 Chop the leeks finely, then cook in a little oil until soft.

6 Beat the eggs together and set a little on one side to use as egg wash. Add the cream to the remainder, strip the tarragon leaves from the stalks and stir into the mixture.

continued overleaf

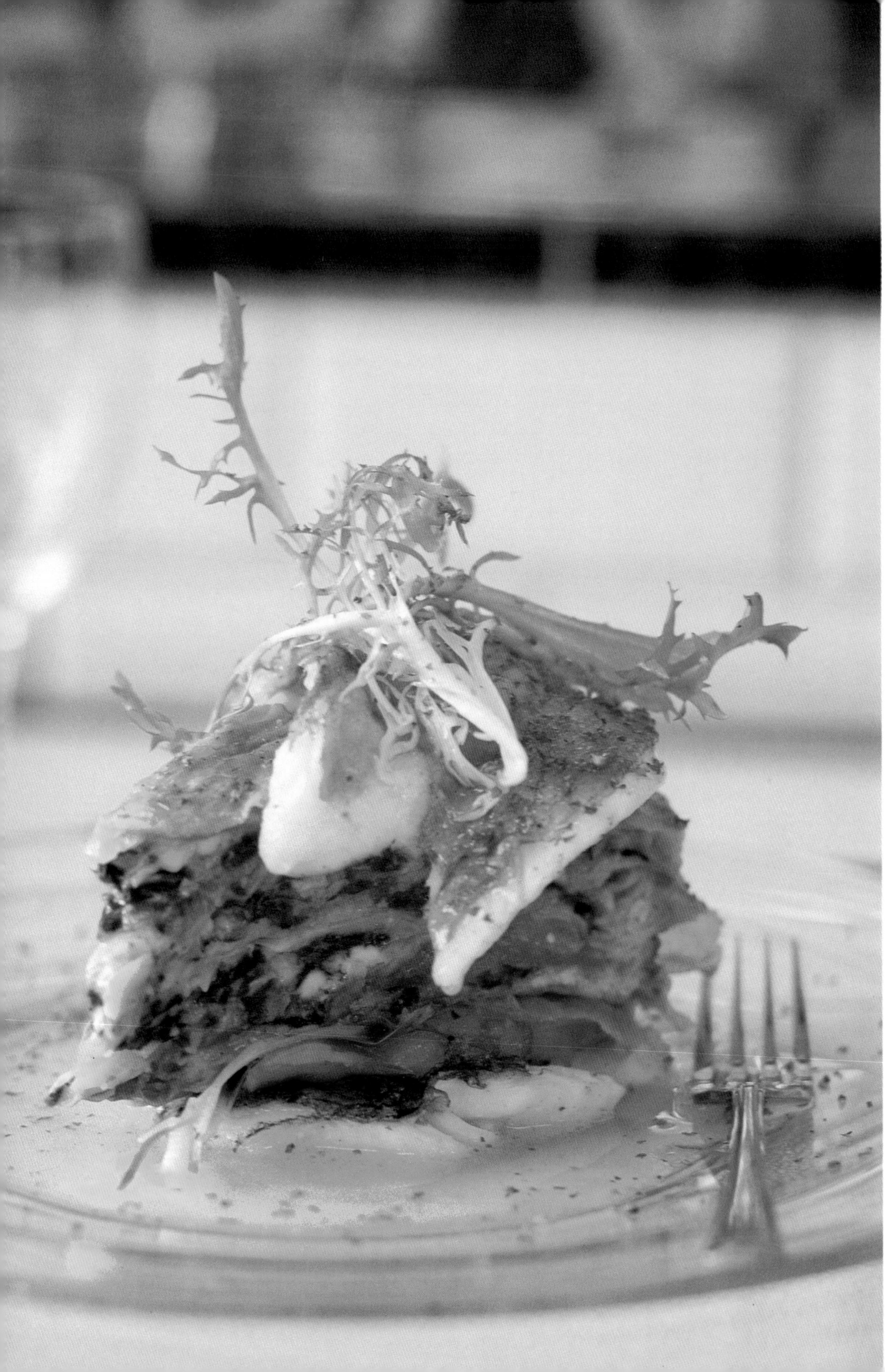

7 Take a 20-cm spring-sided cake tin, and line with 4 sheets of filo pastry, each brushed with melted butter before the next is added.

8 Roll the fillets in seasoned flour and sear them in a pan with a little oil.

9 Fill the pie. Start with 2 or 3 layers of potato – seasoning each layer, then peppers and leeks – mix the colours – then a layer of spinach, then 2 fish fillets. At this point pour on half the egg and cream mix. Top with 2 sheets of filo, glued together with melted butter.

10 Repeat stage 9.

11 Fold in the overhanging 'ears' of filo, and brush with egg wash.

12 Bake in a moderate oven for 50–60 minutes: the top should be nicely browned. Remove. Stand for 5 minutes and take from the tin.

Shopping and showing off

Once again, we are looking for a helpful fishmonger to fillet the John Dory. If unavailable you could substitute other thick white boneless fish fillets – cod, halibut or even coley. Serve with a pool of Pernod Sauce (see page 194)

Tuna with honey-roast chicken wings
and lentil stew

This is a dish that makes much of contrasts: there's the lean and solid tuna, the rich chicken wing meat and the earthy lentils. These multi-layered tastes and textures are all too often the sole preserve of restaurant kitchens, but there's nothing challenging about the techniques involved: follow a succession of simple steps and reap the rewards yourself. Serves four.

50 ml honey

juice of ½ a lemon

25 ml dry white wine

1 dessertspoon paprika

15 cm sprig rosemary

20 ml olive oil

8 chicken wings

25 ml Angostura bitters

25 ml Worcestershire sauce

500 g tuna loin

1 quantity Lentil Stew (see page 201)

1 Preheat your oven to 200°C/ 400°F/gas mark 6.

2 Dissolve the honey into the lemon juice and white wine. Rub it into the chicken wings with the paprika and the leaves torn from the rosemary sprig.

3 Heat the oil in the bottom of an ovenproof pan and seal the chicken wings. Do not let them burn.

4 Transfer the pan to the oven and cook for about 20 minutes, basting occasionally, until the meat is falling off the bone.

5 Shred the meat from the bone and mix with the Angostura and the Worcestershire sauce. Reserve in a warm place.

6 Trim the tuna and cut into 4 portions. Season well and sear in a dry pan: it should be cooked on the outside and very rare inside.

7 Finish off the lentils by heating them through and stirring in the oil and balsamic vinegar.

Shopping and showing off

You could substitute another thick and meat-like fish such as swordfish. To serve, start with the lentils, then add the chicken meat and finally the tuna. Accompany with a green salad.

Seared scallops with red wine pears

This dish looks amazing. The red wine pears have been rescued from their role on the dessert menu, the spicing changed, and then they are teamed up with sweet scallops, and the red wine juices turned into a rich sauce. What's more, it is all very simple to do. Serves four.

4 hard pears

3 cloves

2 cinnamon sticks

peel from 1 large orange

60 g brown sugar

350 ml red wine

8 scallops – the larger the better

50 g chilled butter, plus a little extra

salt and pepper

1 Peel the pears and leave them whole.

2 In a non-reactive saucepan, add the cloves, cinnamon, sugar and orange peel to the red wine. Then add the pears, cover the pan, and poach until cooked (when they are soft to a knife). Remove the pears and keep in a warm place. Strain the cooking liquor and reserve.

3 Smear a heavy frying pan with a minimum of butter, heat it up and sear the scallops, until cooked on the outside – they should be firm, but do not overcook them. Keep in a warm place.

4 Strain the cooking liquor and reduce, if need be, to 120 ml (if cooking the pears has left you short of this amount add a little more red wine). Take the butter straight from the refrigerator so that it is chilled, and cut it into cubes. Whisk it into the sauce which will thicken and become glossy. Adjust the seasoning with salt and pepper.

Shopping and showing off

Ask your fishmonger to clean and prepare the scallops for you. Serve simply: a pool of sauce, with the pear sitting upright and the scallops sliced in half around it.

Fisherman's soup

There has been a great deal written about fish soup, and what started out as a simple dish has acquired enough mystique to become thoroughly daunting. The Livebait philosophy is to take the freshest ingredients, then allow their natural flavours and textures free rein. This recipe is your key to making a genuine fish soup with the minimum of fuss. As the recipe is a succession of simple steps, you don't have to be particularly skilful – just careful.

50 ml olive oil

1 head garlic

1 dessertspoon fennel seeds

a bouquet garni, made by tying together 8 sprigs flat parsley, 4 bay leaves, 6 celery leaves and 4 mint leaves tied up with fine string

1 dessertspoon salt

freshly ground black pepper

75 ml tomato purée

500 g tinned plum tomatoes

1 litre fish stock (see page 186)

500 ml white wine

1 teaspoon paprika

2 small fennel bulbs

250 g potatoes

juice and zest of $\frac{1}{2}$ orange

25 ml Pernod

1 kg mixed white fish – monkfish, turbot, John Dory, brill

$\frac{1}{2}$ g red saffron

1 Take a stockpot with a heavy bottom, and heat the olive oil, add the garlic, peeled and roughly chopped, the fennel seeds, the bouquet garni, the salt and the pepper. Cook gently for 10 minutes.

2 Add the tomato purée, tinned tomatoes, fish stock, wine and paprika. Bring to the boil and simmer for an hour.

3 Remove the bouquet garni and pass the soup through the coarsest blade of a mouli – as a second-best option whoosh it in a food processor but do not allow it to become too fine. Return to the stockpot.

family meals

continued overleaf

4 Cut the fennel bulbs into quarters lengthways, and peel the potatoes then cut them into chunks. Add the fennel, the potatoes, the orange juice and zest, and the Pernod to the pot, then simmer until the potatoes are done – about 15 minutes.

5 Cut the fish into bite-sized chunks. Put the saffron into an egg cup with a little boiling water and steep for 2 minutes. Add the fish and saffron to the pot and simmer for 3–4 minutes until the fish is just cooked.

Shopping and showing off

Omit any single ingredient, except the saffron and the fish stock, and this soup will still be delicious, so feel free to adapt it to suit yourself. You can also pick and choose just which fish to use depending upon availability – after all, that is what fishermen do! Serve in a soup bowl with crusty bread (see page 142–57), and if you are nostalgic for the South of France a dollop of Aïoli (see page 190).

Seared salmon

with potato, coriander and lemon-grass Dauphinoise,
and an artichoke dressing

This takes a simply cooked fillet of salmon and partners it with a new kind of Dauphinoise, and a chunky artichoke dressing which is particularly good. Serves four.

1 globe artichoke

½ lemon

15 ml smooth Dijon mustard

50 ml light olive oil

15 ml balsamic vinegar

salt and pepper

4 × 125 g salmon fillets

1 teaspoon clarified butter

1 quantity Potato, Coriander and Lemon-grass Dauphinoise (see page 203)

1 First prepare the artichoke. Take off two layers of leaves and then slice through horizontally. Trim back to reveal the hairy choke in the centre and remove it with a teaspoon. Rub the trimmed heart all over with half a lemon.

2 Steam the artichoke heart over boiling water until it is tender but not mushy.

3 Cut it into strips and put them in a food processor or blender with the mustard, oil and vinegar, and whoosh for 30 seconds. You are aiming for a chunky consistency not a purée. Put the dressing into a pan and warm gently. Season with salt and pepper.

4 Season the salmon fillets and using the clarified butter sear them in a very hot frying pan. The fillets are done when the outside looks cooked but the very centre is still raw. Take from the pan and allow to rest for 3 minutes.

Shopping and showing off

The best salmon is wild salmon. Better texture. Better taste. But farmed salmon is both more widely available and a good deal cheaper – ask your fishmonger to do the filleting and to remove the pin bones. To bring out the best in this dish put the salmon in the centre of the plate and spoon some of the artichoke dressing over it. Add a wedge of the Dauphinoise or, if more bravura is called for, use a pastry-cutter to ease out a perfect cylinder of the potatoes.

Grilled smoked sturgeon

with 'nero' spinach and paprika sour cream

This stunning dish has just the right combination of textures and flavours, where green vegetables are braised in squid ink and red wine to form a backdrop to plainly grilled fish. So, no ... You cannot make any substitutions. Serves four.

150 g leeks white parts only

50 ml good olive oil

300 g young spinach leaves

100 g curly endive leaves

100 ml chicken stock (see page 188)

100 ml red wine

2 × 25 ml sachets squid ink

salt and pepper

100 ml sour cream

1 tablespoon sweet paprika

4 × 120 g pieces smoked sturgeon

25 g butter

50 g keta salmon caviare (optional)

1 Slice the leeks finely and soften them in the oil in a heavy casserole. Do not allow them to colour.

2 Wash the spinach and the curly endive (use only the white part). Add them to the casserole with the chicken stock and red wine. Braise with the lid on for 30 minutes.

3 Add the squid ink and braise for a further 15 minutes. Take the lid off and stir; the contents should be nearly dry; if still sloppy cook a little longer with the lid off. Season with salt and pepper and keep warm.

4 Mix the sour cream with the paprika and reserve.

5 Take the sturgeon portions and butter them. Cook under a hot grill for 4–5 minutes.

Shopping and showing off

The 'nero' vegetable braise is so original that it makes a good partner for any plainly grilled fish. If you can find the paprika powder made from smoked peppers use it. To serve, start with a foundation of greens, then top with a piece of fish and a dollop of the paprika sour cream. A sprinkling of salmon caviare as garnish adds another element of colour.

Roast monkfish tail

with braised red cabbage

This is comfort food, and about as unfussy as you can get: when it went on the menu at Livebait there was a constant procession of customers asking for the red cabbage recipe. As for all those people who know in their hearts that they should be eating more fish – yes, fish is good for the brain! – this recipe makes a great starting point. It just needs a little mashed potato with it to take care of the juices from the braised red cabbage. Serves four.

80 ml good olive oil

1 bunch fresh tarragon (1 × 15 g supermarket packets)

700 g boned and trimmed monkfish tail

salt and pepper

100 g unsalted butter

150 g shallots

25 g celery leaves

25 g flat parsley

2 bay leaves

1 tablespoon snipped thyme

1 medium red cabbage

200 ml red wine

100 ml freshly squeezed orange juice

200 ml chicken stock (see page 188)

50 g demerara sugar

150 g unsmoked streaky bacon

75 g pitted prunes

40 ml sherry vinegar

1 Make up a marinade from 40 ml of the good olive oil and half the tarragon. Season the monkfish with salt and pepper, then roll it in the marinade. Put on one side for 30 minutes.
2 Put the remaining 40 ml of good olive oil and the butter into a casserole – an iron one that will take direct heat – peel and quarter the shallots and add them with the celery leaves, the rest of the tarragon, the parsley, bay leaves and thyme. Stir until mixed and then put on the lid, turn down the heat and sweat for 10 minutes.
3 Preheat your oven to 220°C/425°F/gas mark 7.

4 Chop the cabbage coarsely and add it to the casserole. Add the red wine, orange juice, chicken stock and sugar. Stir and braise for another 40 minutes with the lid on.

5 Brown the outside of the monkfish in a roasting tray. Take the bacon rashers, and stretch them out using the back of a knife. Wrap them around the sealed monkfish tail. Then roast it for about 25 minutes.

6 Chop the prunes, then add with the sherry vinegar to the cabbage and braise for a further 15 minutes with the lid off. Remove the bay leaves. Taste and adjust seasoning with salt and pepper.

Shopping and showing off

Ask your fishmonger to skin and bone the monkfish tail, although this is a job you can do at home. The dish goes well with some mashed potato, so to present the dish, start with a foundation of mashed potato and red cabbage, then slice the monkfish tail neatly and place 3 slices on each plate – it's as simple as that.

grandstand
dishes

Smoked fish terrine (*see opposite*) 84 Roast fillet of turbot with foie gras mash, braised celery and red wine sauce 86 **Risotto cake with smoked trout, sauce gribiche and roast radicchio 88** 'Millefeuille' of seared bluefin tuna, baba ganoush, red onion jam and baby spinach 90 **Baked whole black bream stuffed with couscous tabbouleh and served with a potato and hazelnut gratin 92** Tiger prawns wrapped in sea bass and roasted, with egg tagliatelle, mussels and Merguez sausage 94 **Roast brill with brandade mash and champagne porcini sauce 96** Tart of mussels in a red curry paste 100 **Crab and wild mushrooms on brioche toast with foie gras vinaigrette 102** Oysters and caramelised leeks, with champagne and strawberry hollandaise sauce 104

Smoked fish terrine

Beautiful to look at, delicious to eat and fiddly to make. Preparing this terrine is quite laborious, but doesn't involve any particularly difficult techniques or obscure ingredients. Take your time, do the job step by step, and you will be delighted with the results. This makes approximately 2 kg of terrine – you'll need a trough about 28 cm long, with a capacity of about 2 litres, and you'll end up with enough terrine for at least twelve large portions.

4 red peppers

4 courgettes

10 ml light olive oil

juice of $\frac{1}{2}$ lemon

600 g potatoes

800 ml fish stock *or* water

bunch of flat parsley (1 × 15 g supermarket pack)

8 sheets gelatine *or* the equivalent in powder

400 g undyed smoked haddock

400 g smoked eel

400 g smoked salmon

salt and pepper

2 quantities Horseradish Cream (see page 192)

1 Preheat your oven to 200°C/400°F/gas mark 6.

2 First things first – preparations. The peppers should be split in half and seeded, then roasted in the oven until just softening – about 20 minutes. Remove and place in a sealed plastic bag. When cool, pull off the skins and cut the peppers into strips about 2 cm wide.

3 Slice the courgettes thinly lengthways. Brush with a little oil and lemon juice, then soften in the oven for about 10 minutes. Allow to cool.

4 Peel and slice the potatoes thinly lengthways, then parboil them in fish stock – they should still be 'crunchy'.

5 Strip the parsley leaves from their stems and reserve.

6 Make up the gelatine with hot water, or a little of the potato water, and put to one side as a 'pot of glue'.

7 Take the terrine, oil it lightly, and line it carefully with a sheet of low-transference clingfilm, which hangs over the edges. This will make turning it out much less of an ordeal.

8 Cut your smoked fish into 50-mm slices working along their length, but at a 45° angle as if you were slicing gravadlax.

9 Remember to season the vegetable layers with salt and pepper as you go, the fish layers just require pepper.

10 Build stage one: a layer of smoked haddock; one of peppers; one of potatoes; one of courgettes; one of flat parsley; seal with a third of the gelatine glue and place in the refrigerator for 20 minutes.

11 Build stage two: a layer of smoked eel; one of peppers; one of potatoes; one of courgettes; one of flat parsley; seal with a third of the gelatine glue and once again place in the refrigerator for 20 minutes.

12 Finally stage three: a layer of smoked salmon; one of peppers; one of potatoes; one of courgettes; one of flat parsley; seal with the last of the gelatine glue. Fold over the clingfilm and place in the refrigerator overnight to set firm.

Shopping and Showing off

Smoked wild salmon is preferable to farmed. If you cannot find smoked eel substitute smoked mackerel. You can replace the leaf gelatine with the powder in sachets, but leaf is easier to handle. When you have turned out the terrine slice it, with a serrated knife, into elegant slices and arrange each on a plate with some green salad leaves and a dollop of Horseradish Cream (see page 192).

Roast fillet of turbot

with foie gras mash, braised celery and red wine sauce

Turbot is the king of fish. Solid, uncompromising flesh, and so rich as to taste almost creamy. Finding a combination of vegetables and a sauce that goes well with such a fish is a taxing problem. This plateful really sings, the opulent mash, the slight crunch of the celery and the rich red wine sauce are all great on their own. With the turbot they are even better. Serves four.

50 g dried porcini mushrooms

700 ml rich red wine

1.5 litres chicken stock (see page 188)

12 celery stalks

1 kg floury potatoes

4 × 350 g turbot fillets

50 ml good olive oil

70 ml sweet white wine

100 g fresh foie gras, prepared by your supplier

50 ml double cream

50 g butter

salt and pepper

1 Soak the porcini with 200 ml of the red wine for 60 minutes

2 Preheat the oven to 220°C/425°F/gas mark 7.

3 Take 1 litre of the chicken stock and boil until reduced by half. Reserve.

4 Take the remaining 500 ml of red wine and boil until reduced to 250 ml.

5 Drain the porcini mushrooms, and pass the red wine they were soaking in through a cloth to remove any grit.

6 Amalgamate the reduced stock, the reduced wine, the mushrooms and the wine they were soaked in. Simmer together for 30–40 minutes.

7 Peel the celery stalks to remove the strings and cut into 3-cm lengths. Put them in a saucepan with the remaining 500 ml of chicken stock, add a teaspoon of salt and cook slowly until they are just done but still a little crunchy. Reserve.

8 Peel and boil the potatoes until they are cooked. Drain and keep warm.

9 Season the turbot fillets, and brush with a little olive oil. Sear in a frying pan to seal, then transfer to a heated roasting dish. Finish in the oven for about 8 minutes. The fish is done when it feels firm and resilient to the touch.

10 Put the sweet white wine into a saucepan and reduce until there are only a couple of tablespoons left. If the foie gras is raw, add it and heat through for 2 minutes. If the foie gras is cooked, take the pan off the heat and then add it.

11 Mash the potatoes with the cream and butter. Add the foie gras and sweet wine from the saucepan, mash to mix well. Season to taste.

Shopping and showing off

Turbot come in two varieties: 'chicken turbot' is the term used for any fish up to about 2 kg, while 'turbot' is reserved for the rarer, larger fish. For this dish the larger the fillets you use the better, twice as many small ones is not really an option. If you cannot get fresh foie gras, then it is more readily available in tins and jars (sometimes described as mi-cuit or bloc de foie gras); unfortunately it is no less expensive. Finely chopped chicken livers will do as a last resort substitute. To present the dish, start with an island of mash surrounded by a sea of mushroom and red wine sauce, top with the fish fillet and finally the celery.

Risotto cake with smoked trout,

sauce gribiche and roast radicchio

At last, a risotto with crispy bits! Pan-frying risotto is a sure way to combine the best of both worlds: on the one hand there is the creamy centre and on the other there is that bit of crunch. Plus this dish delivers the winning combination of sweet-fleshed smoked trout and bitter radicchio. At Livebait the risotto cakes are made individually in small rings and then pushed out as perfect circles. In the home it is easier to make one large cake in a frying pan, then you have the option of punching out a perfect disc of risotto with a pastry cutter and of saving the risotto trimmings to eat the following day – just stir them back to life with a little fresh stock – or you can cut the cake into simple wedges. Serves four.

100 g red onion

100 g yellow pepper

75 ml olive oil

250 g Italian risotto rice

70 ml white wine

bunch tarragon ($\frac{1}{2} \times$ 15 g supermarket pack)

50 g Parmesan

700 ml chicken stock (see page 188)

1 egg

50 ml double cream

salt and pepper

4 small heads radicchio

4 small smoked trout

1 quantity Sauce Gribiche (see page 194)

Pay for your subscription by Direct Debit in easy instalments of just **£15.00** every 6 months – that's the equivalent of 12 issues for the price of 10.

See overleaf for full details

Subscribe

and receive **2 FREE** issues

1 Preheat your oven to 200°C/400°F/gas mark 6.

2 Dice the onion and pepper finely and cook in a deep saucepan with 50 ml of the olive oil until soft. Add the rice and cook for a minute or two.

3 Add the wine and stir until it is all absorbed.

4 Warm the chicken stock and stir into the rice mixture a ladleful at a time, only proceeding when the previous quantity has been absorbed.

5 When all the stock is incorporated take the pan off the heat and allow to cool down.

6 Grate the Parmesan finely, and beat it with the egg and the cream. Stir into the risotto, which should end up quite firm, not sloppy.

7 Peel the radicchio to leave neat hearts, brush with oil and roast in the oven for 10 minutes.

8 Transfer the risotto mixture to a deep frying pan and cook until a good crisp skin has formed. Lift the edge of the cake up with a palette knife to check.

9 Then put the pan under a hot grill to crisp up the top of the cake.

10 Take the smoked trout. Turn them over on their backs and snip through the backbone just by the head and just by the tail – you should be able to pull the bone free (and all the pin bones should come with it), leaving a boneless fish that still has its head and tail.

Shopping and showing off

You can use any medium grain rice, but a genuine risotto rice, like Arborio or Carnoli is preferable. Smoked trout are readily available at supermarkets, and if you don't want to go so far as the 'head and tail' presentation outlined here, smoked trout fillets will suffice. Cut the risotto cake into 4 wedges. Place one on a plate, and top with a trout. Surround with Sauce Gribiche then garnish with a roasted radicchio head split into 4.

'Millefeuille' of seared bluefin tuna,

baba ganoush, red onion jam and baby spinach

This makes a fine dinner party starter, fish course or even centrepiece. Make the 'biscuit' element of the Millefeuille in whatever size and shape suits your presentation but remember that, in the home kitchen, larger is generally easier. Both the Baba Ganoush and the Red Onion Jam need to be prepared ahead of time. The recipe serves four, based on four 'biscuits' each, when each biscuit is about 5 cm square.

1 × 500 g packet butter puff pastry

1 egg

400 g bluefin tuna loin

salt and pepper

200 g baby spinach

25 ml good olive oil

1 quantity Baba Ganoush (see page 198–9)

1 quantity Red Onion Jam (see page 182)

watercress to garnish

1 Preheat your oven to 200°C/400°F/gas mark 6.

2 Start by making the 'biscuits'. Roll out the butter puff pastry until it is 25 mm thick. Mark out into 16 biscuits, with the back of a knife, scoring the pastry fairly deeply but not cutting right through it.

3 Beat the egg and use it to glaze the biscuits. Then arrange them on a baking tray lined with baking parchment.

3 Bake in the oven for 15–20 minutes. Cool on a rack, then cut into biscuits.

4 Heat a frying pan with just the merest dab of oil, season the tuna. Then sear it on all sides. It should be cooked on the outside and raw in the middle.

5 Cut the seared tuna into 12 equal slices.

6 To assemble: put a tiny smear of Baba Ganoush on the plate to glue everything in place, and add a pastry biscuit glazed side up; then take one of the tuna slices, brush with olive oil and lay out on the biscuit; then a few leaves of spinach; then a biscuit; then a tuna slice brushed with oil; then a layer of Red Onion Jam; then a biscuit; then a tuna slice brushed with oil; then a layer of Baba Ganoush; then a final biscuit glazed side up. Watercress makes the best garnish.

Shopping and showing off

Ready-made *butter* puff pastry is not at all bad, but standard supermarket puff pastry often disappoints. If your fishmonger doesn't have any bluefin tuna you could substitute fresh raw salmon – it's worth getting wild salmon if you can, as the texture is so much better. If you find yourself making the Red Onion Jam and Baba Ganoush just for this recipe, the Bread section (see pages 142–57) will help you use up any surplus.

Baked whole black bream

stuffed with couscous tabbouleh and served with a potato and hazelnut gratin

The black bream is a tasty and much underrated fish, and serving an individual fish to each diner is certainly a show stopper. Serves four.

200 g couscous

juice of 1 orange

75 ml olive oil, plus a little extra

½ red pepper

½ yellow pepper

½ bunch spring onions

2 plum tomatoes

1 courgette

1 cucumber

salt and pepper

2 teaspoons harissa paste

4 × 350 g black bream

1 quantity Potato and Hazelnut Gratin (see page 38)

watercress or leaves to garnish

1 Preheat your oven to 200°C/400°F/gas mark 6.

2 Half cook the couscous in boiling salted water – this will take about 10 minutes.

3 Warm the orange juice in a non-reactive saucepan, add the couscous and 50 ml of olive oil, stir, cover the pot with clingfilm and put to one side in a warm place for an hour or more.

4 Prepare all the vegetables (to skin the peppers toast them under a grill until black, then leave in a sealed plastic bag until cool – the skins will rub off), then dice. Chop the spring onions; peel, seed and chop the tomatoes; dice the courgettes; peel, seed and dice the cucumber.

5 Season the vegetable mix, then dissolve the harissa paste in the remaining 25 ml of olive oil and drizzle over the vegetables.

6 Crumble the couscous by hand, and mix with the vegetables.

7 Take each fish and use scissors to snip through the backbone close to the head and again at the tail. Press down on the bone, then pull away the backbone and the pin bones. Stuff the cavity with the couscous mixture and 'stitch' up the belly with a thin, oiled, bamboo satay skewer.

8 Oil the fish, then season and roast for 25 minutes in a hot oven Serve with Potato and Hazelnut Gratin (see page 38)

Shopping and showing off

Harissa is a concentrated pungent chilli paste from North Africa and you'll find it at delicatessens and supermarkets – it is well worth keeping in the store cupboard.

Plate each fish and garnish with watercress or other dark green leaves. Place a wedge of Potato and Hazelnut Gratin to one side.

Tiger prawns wrapped in sea bass

and roasted, with egg tagliatelle, mussels and Merguez sausage

This dish looks good and tastes good too. The egg tagliatelle with mussels and Merguez sausage makes it substantial and there is an invaluable 'surprise' spicy flavour in the lurking Merguez sausage. Serves four.

4 extra large raw tiger prawns

4 × 200 g sea bass fillets

25 ml olive oil

salt and pepper

1 quantity Egg Tagliatelle with Mussels and Merguez Sausage (see page 40)

1 Preheat your oven to 170°C/335°F/gas mark 3½.

2 Carefully peel the tail part of the shell from the prawns, being careful to leave the head attached. Run a knife down the back of each prawn to remove the dark vein.

3 Season your sea bass fillets and wrap each one carefully round the tail of a prawn – leaving the head poking out, as if the prawn were in a giant sleeping bag. Secure the parcel with a cocktail stick to prevent it unravelling. Brush with olive oil.

4 Place upright on a baking sheet and roast in the oven for 8–10 minutes.

Shopping and showing off

Tiger prawns are widely available, but do try to get large ones – failing these you can substitute langoustines but they must be raw. Ask your fishmonger nicely and he'll fillet and pin-bone the sea bass. To serve, simply position your prawn-crowned fillet on the top of a hillock of the Tagliatelle.

Roast brill with brandade mash

and champagne porcini sauce

Brill is a very finely flavoured fish, but it does need a little bit of help. The rich and substantial Brandade Mash (see page 26) goes very well, as does the champagne porcini sauce. Serves four.

30 g dried porcini (ceps)

1 quantity Brandade Mash (see page 26)

50 g shallots

20 ml light olive oil

1 bunch fresh tarragon (1 × 15 g supermarket pack)

500 ml chicken stock

250 ml champagne

70 ml double cream

1 × 1.5–2 kg brill, filleted

salt and pepper

1 Cover the porcini in warm water and leave them to rehydrate for at least an hour.

2 Preheat your oven to 220°C/425°F/gas mark 7.

3 If you are using leftover Brandade Mash, put it into a gratin dish and place in the bottom of the oven to warm through.

4 Chop the shallots and sweat in a little of the oil. Drain the mushrooms, saving the water but straining it through a cloth to remove any grit. Then add the mushrooms to the pan. Fry everything together for 3–4 minutes.

5 Add the mushroom water and reduce by half.

6 Strip the tarragon leaves from their stalks and add them. Add the stock and reduce by half.

7 Add three-quarters of the champagne and reduce by half.

8 Add the cream and reduce until the sauce coats the back of a spoon.

9 Take off the heat and keep warm.

10 Season the brill fillets and seal on both sides in a hot pan with a little oil.

11 Roast in the oven for 6–7 minutes. They are cooked when resilient to the touch.

12 Meanwhile finish the sauce: add the remaining champagne, stir and adjust the seasoning.

Shopping and showing off

If you jib at cooking with champagne (despite the fact you get a cast-iron excuse to drink the remaining four glasses from the bottle), *méthode champenoise,* or *cava* will do fine. Turbot makes a splendid stand-in if you cannot get brill. Serve by piling a mound of the wonderful Brandade Mash centrally, topping it with a brill fillet and adding a moat of Champagne Porcini Sauce.

Tart of mussels in a red curry paste

This is a Thai-inspired red curry paste and, as with all curry pastes, its exact composition is subject to the availability of the various ingredients. At Livebait we use more chillies, and add some coriander root, which gives a very concentrated flavour. Take the recipe here and use it as a starting point for your own experiments. These quantities will make two 20-cm tarts, which would serve eight.

100 g garlic

100 g red onions

40 g galangal

100 g lemon grass

3 fat red chillies

juice of 2 limes

50 g 'blachan' – shrimp paste

1 teaspoon powdered cinnamon

1 teaspoon pink peppercorns

1 teaspoon cumin seeds

1 teaspoon coriander powder

1 teaspoon sweet paprika

60 ml coconut milk

60 ml sake *or* dry sherry

60 g sweet potato

750 g mussels

1 bunch fresh coriander

75 g crème fraîche

2 eggs

400 g butter, shortcrust pastry

1 Preheat your oven to 180°C/350°F/gas mark 4½.

2 Peel and chop the garlic, onions, galangal, lemon grass and chillies. Then add them with the lime juice, shrimp paste and spices to a food processor or blender. While the machine is running, add enough water (70 ml or so) to make a paste.

3 Put the paste into a pan and heat gently. Add the coconut milk and sake and reduce by half.

4 Roll out the pastry until it is about 5 mm thick, and use it to line two 20-cm diameter flan tins. Blind bake the pastry cases by putting a sheet of greased baking parchment into each, and weighting it with dried beans. Put them in the oven for 15 minutes. Remove, discard the paper and beans, brush the inside with beaten egg and return to the oven for 5 minutes. The tarts are then ready for their filling.

5 Peel and dice the sweet potato and cook until done (about 20 minutes).

6 Steam the mussels briefly and pick out the meat, omitting any which do not open. Chop the coriander leaves. Add the mussels and coriander to the cooling red sauce mix.

7 Beat the crème fraîche with the eggs and stir into the mix.

8 Fill the pastry cases with the mixture and return them to the oven for 30 minutes.

Shopping and showing off

Anything you do not immediately recognise on the ingredients list can probably be found at any shop specialising in Thai provisions. And such has been the recent surge in popularity of Thai dishes that many of the large supermarkets will have them too. You may prefer to make a number of individual tartlets rather than two large tarts, but either way a salad of crisp green leaves would make the perfect accompaniment.

Crab and wild mushrooms

on brioche toast with foie gras vinaigrette

This is an assemblage, but a very cunning one. The crab is very rich, and the mushrooms provide a different texture – as does the toast. Let the wild mushrooms be chanterelles, although whatever your supermarket can supply, up to and including reconstituted ceps, will do. Serves four.

1 quantity Foie Gras Vinaigrette (see page 192)

1 pink grapefruit

150 g leeks, from the white part

50 ml good olive oil

300 g chanterelles *or* other wild mushrooms

60 ml dry white wine

1 bunch fresh tarragon (1 × 15 g supermarket pack)

1 bunch spring onions, finely chopped

500 g white, hand-picked crab meat

salt and pepper

4 slices brioche

1 Make the Foie Gras Vinaigrette in advance and cut the grapefruit into segments removing all pith and skin.

2 Chop the leeks finely, then soften them in a lidded casserole, with the oil.

3 Brush the mushrooms to get rid of grit, chop them roughly and add them and the white wine to the casserole. Strip the tarragon leaves from the stems and add them.

4 Put on the lid, turn down to a simmer and cook for 15–20 minutes.

5 Finely chop the spring onions and add, then stir in the crab. Adjust the seasoning, and keep warm.

6 Toast the brioche.

Shopping and showing off

500 g of picked crab meat is roughly what you would get from a 2 kg cock crab. By all means take a short-cut and get the crab ready-picked from your fishmonger, but do be sure that the crab meat is fresh, not pasteurised. For presentation, start with a slice of brioche toast and top with the crab and mushroom mixture, then add the grapefruit segments. Dress with the Foie Gras Vinaigrette (see page 192). Either buy a brioche or make your own (see page 156), or even get away with a slice of good wholemeal toast, well buttered.

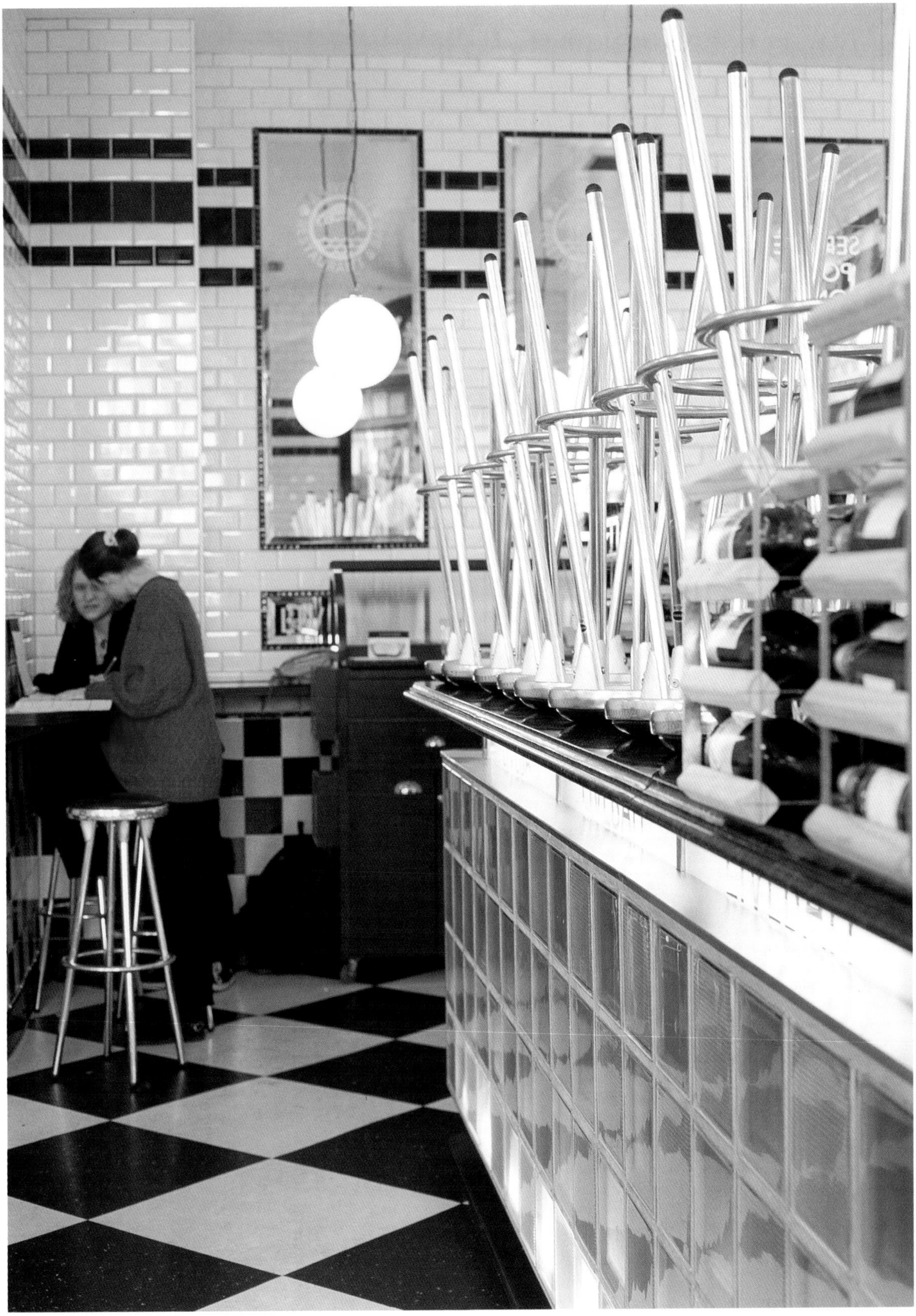

Oysters and caramelised leeks,

with champagne and strawberry hollandaise sauce

It's easy to forget how acid strawberries are. In this dish they provide a welcome bite to a champagne hollandaise sauce. The oysters are poached to firm them up, and the leeks cooked to bring out their sweetness. This is a great dish to show off with, but you do need a hand blender and a thermometer. Serves four.

300 g leeks, white parts only

$\frac{1}{2}$ small red chilli

50 g salted butter

6 strawberries

$\frac{1}{2}$ lemon

12 large rock oysters

100 ml white wine

100 ml champagne

15 ml white wine vinegar

1 teaspoon pickled green peppercorns

4 egg yolks

250 g lukewarm clarified butter

salt and pepper

1 Chop the leeks finely, seed and chop the red chilli very finely. Place them in a saucepan with the salted butter and cook slowly for 30 minutes. The leeks should be reduced to a rich, caramelised mass. Reserve.

2 Make a strawberry purée in your food processor: whoosh the strawberries and adjust the taste with lemon juice.

3 Open the oysters (unless you have inveigled your fishmonger into doing this job for you! Remember to ask for the shells and juice).

4 Remove the meat and save the liquid from the oysters. Mix the oyster juice with the white wine and boil for 3 minutes until the alcohol has gone.

5 Allow to cool down to 70°C – check with a thermometer – then 'poach' the oysters for 3 minutes without allowing the liquid to boil. Do not overcook and the oysters will stay plump. Remove and allow to cool.

6 Put the champagne, vinegar and peppercorns in a saucepan and reduce over a low heat until you have about 60 ml of liquid. Cool.

7 When cool add the egg yolks and use a hand blender to mix thoroughly. Put the saucepan on to a minimal heat and continue to blend. The sauce should grow in volume and become fluffy and light. Do NOT exceed 60°C or you will have scrambled eggs!

8 Remove from the stove, continue to blend and gradually add the cool clarified butter, then add the strawberry purée. Season with salt and pepper.

9 Take half of the deep oyster shells and fill each with: a layer of caramelised leek, 1 oyster meat, a thick coating of champagne and strawberry hollandaise. Then finish under a hot grill, being careful that the hollandaise doesn't burn.

Shopping and showing off

Opening oysters is easier than it looks: ask for a demo at the fishmonger's, get an oyster knife and start practising. At Livebait, we serve 3 shells which makes a good portion, and the dish is made even more extravagant by the addition of a dollop of Sevruga caviare.

dinners
à deux

Tartare of home-salted cod, avocado and radish fool, with an egg yolk *(see opposite)* 108   Tuna au poivre with Szechuan pickled cucumbers and black shiitake mushrooms 111   **Brill with seared scallops and a casserole of summer vegetables 112**   Honey and ginger roast octopus 114 **Scallops with vegetable tagine 117**   Spring rolls of squid, oyster and bacon with curly endive and shiitake mushrooms, apple and sultana chutney 118 **Grilled salmon on an artichoke 'pizza' with tomatoes and feta cheese 120**   Scallops with roast quince and cardoon 122   **Lobster, Jersey Royal potato salad with pleurotte mushrooms, salmon caviare and gazpacho sauce 124**

Tartare of home-salted cod, avocado and radish fool, with an egg yolk

This dish provides a succession of contrasting textures. The avocado fool is a smooth green purée with chunks of peppery radish bobbing around like early naval mines, while the home-cured cod is firm and somehow tastes fresher than fresh! The only drawback is that the dish does need planning: it will never be the star of an impromptu meal. Serves two with cod left over – which will be splendid in sandwiches or on toast.

1 fat red chilli

1 bunch flat-leafed parsley (1 × 15 g supermarket pack)

250 g granulated sugar

80 g sea salt

1 kg thick fillet of cod, pin-boned – ask your fishmonger

100 ml double cream

juice of ½ lemon

1 ripe avocado

2 spring onions

salt and pepper

½ bunch radishes

25 ml good olive oil

2 egg yolks

100 g cornichons

100 g caperberries

1 teaspoon sweet paprika

1 To cure the cod. Finely chop the chilli and flat parsley, mix with the sugar and salt. Cover the bottom of a plastic container (one that has a lid) with a third of the mixture. Put the cod fillet on the salt mix, skin side down. Cover with the rest of the mixture. Leave for 24 hours with the lid on in the refrigerator (unless yours gets colder than 6°C – if the cod gets very cold it starts to freeze, which inhibits the curing process). Turn the fish once.

2 To make the fool, place the cream and lemon juice in your food-processor – or liquidiser – and whoosh until the cream is whipped to stiff peaks. This is important as the whipped cream will give the fool its lightness.

3 Dice the avocado, chop the spring onions and add them as you continue to whoosh.

4 Season with salt and freshly ground black pepper.

5 Rinse the cod thoroughly and slice it as thinly as possible on the bias – in the same way that you would cut gravadlax or smoked salmon.

Shopping and showing off

Cod: make your fishmonger work for his money – you want it from the thick end and you want the pin bones removed. Eggs: it is still the advice of the government that we do not eat raw eggs, which is a pity as the egg yolk lubricates the whole dish wonderfully. If you disagree with the official line and wish to take the responsibility on yourself, use really good fresh eggs that are free-range and come from a flock certified free of salmonella, otherwise omit the egg yolk. Start with a dollop of fool on each plate. Cut the radishes into quarters and embed them in the fool. Top with a fan of sliced cod. Paint with olive oil so that it glistens prettily and sit an unbroken egg yolk on the very top. Chop the cornichons and scatter them with the caperberries around the edges of the plate. Drizzle over some olive oil and use the paprika to add colour.

Tuna au poivre

with Szechuan pickled cucumbers
and black shiitake mushrooms

Treating loin of tuna like meat makes a lot of sense: it is solid, best eaten rare and carries a strong flavour well. Ask your fishmonger for a nice chunk of loin of tuna without the belly piece. Make the cucumber and mushroom pickle a day or two in advance and this sophisticated dish comes together very quickly indeed. Serves two.

70 g mixed peppercorns – green, black, pink and white

400 g loin of tuna

salt

a smear of light olive oil

1 quantity Szechuan Pickled Cucumbers and Black Shiitake Mushrooms (see page 184–5)

1 Preheat your oven to 220°C/425°F/gas mark 7.

2 Crack the peppercorns in pestle and mortar, or failing that use a coffee grinder. They need to be in small pieces but not turned to dust.

3 Salt the whole piece of tuna, then roll it in the peppercorn mixture – press the cracked pepper into the fish.

4 Get a heavy pan very hot and lubricate with a minimum of olive oil.

5 Press each surface of the tuna on to the hot pan. By the time you have finished, the fish will be almost cooked. Transfer to the oven for 2–3 minutes. The objective is for the tuna to remain very rare in the centre.

6 Rest for a further 5 minutes, then slice.

Shopping and showing off

Buy tuna just as you would go about buying steak: it's expensive, it's a treat, it should be chosen and handled with care. Find a good fishmonger and trust him. Multi-coloured peppercorns may be had at supermarkets prepacked in jars. To serve, arrange the slices of tuna carefully and surround with the Szechuan pickle.

Brill with seared scallops

and a casserole of summer vegetables

A delicious dish, and one where you have some flexibility. Peas and broad beans form the basis for this casserole of fresh vegetables, but you could mix and match with other ingredients like artichoke hearts and asparagus. The casserole should be very sloppy and a foil for the solid brill and tender scallops. Serves two.

200 g shallots

3 garlic cloves

1 bunch fresh dill (1 × 15 g supermarket pack)

$\frac{1}{2}$ bunch fresh parsley ($\frac{1}{2}$ × 15 g supermarket pack)

100 ml good olive oil

3 plum tomatoes

250 g broad beans in the pod *or* 100 g frozen

250 g peas in the pod *or* 100 g frozen

1 artichoke heart (optional)

300 ml water

juice of $\frac{1}{2}$ lemon

salt and pepper

200 g asparagus spears (optional)

2 × 250 g brill fillets

50 g flour

100 ml light olive oil

4 fresh scallops

1 bunch fresh basil (a pot from the supermarket)

1 Peel the shallots and leave whole; peel and crush 2 garlic cloves; chop half of the dill and all of the parsley. Add everything to an iron casserole pot with 50 ml of the good olive oil. Heat gently, and sweat with the lid on for 15 minutes, until the shallots begin to soften.

2 Peel, seed and chop the tomatoes. Add them to the casserole. Pod the broad beans and peas and add them. Add the artichoke heart (if you are using one), plus the water, the lemon juice, and 2 teaspoons of salt. Cover and cook gently for 25 minutes. Add the asparagus (if you are using any) and cook for a final 3 minutes. Keep warm.

3 Season the brill and roll in flour. Pan fry in the 100 ml of light olive oil, for approximately 5 minutes until the fish is firm and cooked.

4 Sear the scallops in an almost dry pan until just cooked.

5 Make up the dressing by liquidising the remaining 50 ml of good olive oil, the last garlic clove, the basil, and the remaining dill. Adjust seasoning with salt.

Shopping and showing off

While not ideal, this dish will work with frozen vegetables. It should be served in soup bowls; ladle in the vegetable mixture, add a crisply fried brill fillet and dress each portion with 2 scallops. Drizzle a little of the dressing over the fish.

Honey and ginger roast octopus

This is a typical Livebait dish, at first glance very simple but also quite intricate and the octopus keeps its character. Serve it with a crisp Salade Niçoise – this is one they wouldn't recognise in Nice! Serves two.

1 litre water

1 litre malt vinegar

750 ml cheap red wine

4 bay leaves

10 coriander seeds

10 black peppercorns

50 g root ginger

1 kg cleaned octopus

5 tablespoons runny honey

juice of 3 limes

1 fat red chilli

25 g crystallised ginger

1 quantity Salade Niçoise (see page 28)

1 Take a large stainless steel saucepan (aluminium or other reactive pans may leave a 'taint'). Add the water, vinegar, wine, bay leaves, coriander seeds and peppercorns. Peel the root ginger and add in 2-cm chunks.

2 Add the octopus and bring to the boil, reduce to a simmer until cooked – which is when the point of a knife slips easily into it – about an hour. Lift the octopus out and discard the liquid.

3 Preheat your oven to 200°C/400°F/gas mark 6.

4 Dissolve the honey in the lime juice by warming them together in a stainless steel pan. Add the chilli, chopped finely – discard the seeds if you do not like your dishes hot – and the crystallised ginger, chopped very finely.

5 Cut the octopus into manageable pieces and use a pastry brush to paint them with the warm marinade.

6 Put the octopus into a roasting tin and roast in a hot oven for 15 minutes: overcooking will make it tough.

continued overleaf

Shopping and showing off

First choice is the kind of octopus known as a 'red' octopus. These come from the Mediterranean and Aegean seas, and can be distinguished from the Atlantic octopus as they have a double row of suckers on each tentacle. Octopus can be bought at good fishmongers or in some supermarkets, usually deep frozen and in 1 kg blocks. For this dish frozen octopus is a perfectly good option. Once you have boiled the octopus it will keep in a refrigerator for up to 3 days before you roast it. To serve, pile the warm octopus in the middle of a plate and arrange the Salade Niçoise in a ring around it – sprinkle a little extra dressing on to the salad.

Scallops with vegetable tagine

Time for something that is both simple and exotic. Spicy, slightly crunchy vegetables perfectly complement the sweet but firm scallop meat. Any tagine left over should be saved for bread making (see page 149). Serves two.

100 g onions

1 dessertspoon light olive oil

100 g carrots

100 g fennel

100 g parsnips

100 g courgettes

1 dessertspoon Chermoula (see page 181)

500 ml chicken stock

4 scallops

1 quantity Harissa Vinaigrette (see page 193)

1 Slice the onions, take a heavy saucepan and cook them until soft in the oil.

2 Peel the vegetables and cut them into batons about 4 cm long by 1 cm square.

3 Add the Chermoula to the pan, stir in the vegetables and fry the mixture. As they start to colour, add the chicken stock.

4 Simmer for 25 minutes, or until all the stock is absorbed. Keep warm.

5 Season the scallops with sea salt and freshly ground black pepper, and sear them in a hot pan – they are done when they are firm to the touch. Try to avoid overcooking them.

Shopping and showing off

You should ask your fishmonger for the largest fresh scallops: he will be happy to clean them for you. If they are monsters – shells about 20 cm across – slice them in half. Frozen scallops will do, but defrost them conscientiously and pat them dry. Arrange a pile of tagine on each plate then add two scallops, and drizzle over some Harissa Vinaigrette for a bit more bite.

dinners à deux

117

Spring rolls of squid, oyster and bacon

with curly endive and shiitake mushrooms, apple and sultana chutney

These seriously tasty spring rolls come with an elegant side salad topped with the tentacles of the squid grilled until crisp. While you need to be neat and methodical in your approach no special techniques are required. Serves two.

50 g dried shiitake mushrooms

300 g cleaned squid including tentacles

70 g smoked bacon

6 opened oysters

squeeze of lemon juice

1 bunch spring onions

25 ml light olive oil

100 ml crème fraîche

salt and pepper

6 sheets ready-made filo pastry

50 g melted butter

1 egg

1 head curly endive (frisée)

1 quantity Balsamic vinaigrette (see page 193)

1 quantity Apple and Sultana Chutney (see page 186)

1 Preheat your oven to 220°C/425°F/gas mark 7.

2 Soak the mushrooms in warm water for at least an hour.

3 Cut the squid bodies into large dice (about 2 cm square), put the tentacles on one side.

4 Cut the rind from the bacon, and chop into small dice.

5 Poach the oysters until just firming up – about 1 minute in simmering water which has had a squeeze of lemon juice added – remove with a slotted spoon.

6 Chop the spring onions and fry them off in a little oil with the bacon. After 5 minutes, add the bits of squid body, and the mushrooms, drained and chopped roughly. Stir and cook for a further 2 minutes.

7 Allow the mixture to cool, then add the oysters and crème fraîche. Adjust the seasoning.

8 Lay out a sheet of filo, paint with melted butter and then top with a second sheet. Cut the sheets down the middle. Each narrow strip will make a spring roll.

9 Place a dollop of mixture on the sheet and roll, turning the edges in to make a spring roll. There should be 6 in all.

10 Put the spring rolls on a greased baking sheet, and beat an egg. Paint the spring rolls with the egg wash and bake for 8–10 minutes.

11 Meanwhile brush the tentacles with olive oil, and cook until crisp under the grill.

Shopping and showing off

Fishmongers in Britain tend to pander to their customers' prejudices by discarding the tentacles when selling squid. This is a shame as tentacles are wonderful when crisped up. Insist on getting yours. To serve, make a nest of the curly endive leaves, fill with the three spring rolls and top with the tentacles. Drizzle all over with Balsamic Vinaigrette, and add a dollop of apple and sultana chutney on the side of the plate.

Grilled salmon on an artichoke 'pizza'
with tomatoes and feta cheese

This is a luxurious dish that, on inspection, proves to be surprisingly healthy. The salmon is plainly grilled, while the dough element of a real pizza has been replaced with an artichoke heart. The sauce is simply the liquid the artichoke has been cooked in. Fish, vegetables, olive oil and a little cheese – the perfect Mediterranean combination. Serves two.

2 globe artichokes

1 lemon

250 ml medium sweet white wine

6 plum tomatoes

2 cloves garlic

100 g flat parsley leaves

salt and pepper

1 bunch fresh basil (1 × 15g supermarket plant in a pot)

2 × 150 g pieces of salmon fillet

25 ml good olive oil

100 g soft feta cheese

1 First prepare the artichokes. Take off two layers of leaves and then slice through horizontally. Trim back to reveal the hairy choke in the centre and remove it with a teaspoon, be sure you leave a bowl-shaped depression in the centre of each heart. Halve the lemon and rub the trimmed hearts with one half, then put them into water with the juice from the whole lemon to stop them going dark.

2 Put the white wine in a saucepan, and boil intensively to drive off the alcohol – this should take 3–4 minutes.

3 Drain the artichokes upside down on kitchen paper.

4 Core, skin and seed the plum tomatoes, chop them roughly. Chop the garlic cloves, and the parsley. Put it all into a heavy, lidded pan with the reduced wine and a teaspoon of salt. Stir, and sit the artichokes in the mixture. Put the lid on and cook very slowly for about 25 minutes or until the artichokes are tender.

5 Tear the basil leaves into strips, add them to the pot, and remove from the heat, check the seasoning.

6 Season the salmon, then oil and cook it under a hot grill for 3 minutes a side, skin side first.

7 At the same time, use the other side of your grill pan to finish the artichokes. Use a slotted spoon to remove them from the sauce, then pop some of the tomato pieces into the depression in the middle of each, drizzle with a little olive oil, sprinkle with the feta and grill.

8 Season the remaining juices with salt and pepper.

Shopping and showing off

Any robust white wine will do, at Livebait we make this dish with an Alsatian Riesling. Ready-prepared supermarket salmon portions will do fine. To serve, simply balance the salmon on the top of the artichoke and surround with the tomatoey cooking juices.

Scallops with roast quince and cardoon

This dish provides an amazing combination of tastes and textures: the sweetness of the scallops, the tang of the quince and the salty crunch of the cardoon. Take heart in the face of such obscure fruit and vegetables: a pear will easily stand in for a quince, and you can substitute red Swiss chard or celery for the cardoons. If you have a helpful greengrocer, do try the dish in all its glory, you will find it well worth the effort. Serves two.

2 quinces *or* pears

100 ml white wine

40 g honey

1 small onion

25 ml olive oil

1 head cardoon *or* ruby chard *or* celery

300 ml white wine

300 ml chicken stock (see page 188)

4 large scallops

juice of 2 lemons

rind of 1 lemon

150 g butter, cold from the refrigerator

salt

1 Preheat your oven to 180°C/ 350°F/gas mark 4½.

2 Mix the white wine and honey. Then peel and core the quinces and paint with the mixture.

2 Roast on a tray in the oven for 2 hours – or 20–30 minutes if you are using pears. Put to one side.

3 Peel the onion and chop finely, cook with a little oil in a large saucepan until translucent.

4 Peel the cardoon or celery to remove the strings. If you're using Swiss chard trim it carefully. Cut into 4-cm lengths and add to the saucepan, with the wine and chicken stock.

5 Simmer for between 60 and 80 minutes for cardoons or celery, and just 45 minutes for Swiss chard. Drain, and reserve the vegetables and the cooking liquid. All of the above may be done well in advance of finishing the dish.

6 Put the quince or pear, and the cardoon, celery or chard, into a slow oven to warm through while you sear the scallops in a lightly oiled, heavy pan. Do not overcook them: they are done when they are firm to the touch. Reserve, while you make the sauce.

7 Put the lemon juice and rind into a pan, and heat up. Add 50 ml of the cardoon cooking liquid. Reduce the pan juices by a third . Cut the butter into small cubes, and add them a couple at a time while whisking. The sauce should be thickened and glossy. Adjust the seasoning.

Shopping and showing off

You should ask your fishmonger for large fresh scallops – allow 2 per person. Frozen scallops will do, but defrost them conscientiously and pat them dry. Arrange the quince in the centre of the plate, with the cardoons, chard or celery to one side. If they are very large scallops cut each one into three slices and 'shingle' them. Surround with the sauce.

Lobster, Jersey Royal potato salad
with pleurotte mushrooms, salmon caviare
and gazpacho sauce

It seems as if every year a murmur goes around the foodie community that, 'This year the Jersey Royals are not what they were.' But every year they provide a foretaste of summer, and every year they turn out to be delicious. The waxiness of the potatoes teams up well with the sweetness of the lobster, and the dressing made with fresh dill is worth filing away for use with any sweet fish or shellfish. This is a dish to share, and it serves two people.

200 g Jersey Royal potatoes

50 ml light olive oil

50 ml sweet sherry

20 g shallots

50 g pleurotte mushrooms

salt and pepper

1 × 1 kg cooked lobster

½ bunch fresh dill (½ × 15 g supermarket pack)

20 ml good olive oil

20 ml sherry vinegar

50 g salmon caviare

1 quantity Gazpacho Sauce (see page 196)

1 Wash the potatoes and leave the skins on. If there are any very large ones cut them in half. Cook the potatoes in boiling water – no salt – until they are half cooked. Strain.

2 Put the olive oil into a frying pan and heat it up until smoking. Add the potatoes and stir as they seal.

3 As the potatoes cook, add the sherry and allow to reduce and caramelise.

4 Turn down the heat and cook until the potatoes are nearly done – they should have a tiny bit of 'bite' to them. Stir in the raw shallots, finely chopped, and finally the pleurottes, which will cook very quickly.

5 Cool to lukewarm before seasoning with salt and pepper to taste.

Shopping and showing off

Supermarket lobsters are perfectly OK, but (as with all fish) fresher is always better. So if you can get a live lobster and boil it yourself, or one that's straight from a fishmonger's pot, do so. If you end up with a frozen precooked lobster do not despair: they need a little 'help' and this is just the recipe to make one shine. If you are the sort of person who won't have sweet sherry in the house simply add a dessertspoon of brown sugar to the dry sherry. Pleurotte mushrooms are also called oyster mushrooms. Salmon caviare is widely available and sometimes called keta. Split the lobster and take the shell off the tail section, leave the head on, and crack the claw. Snip the dill finely, and mix with the olive oil and sherry vinegar. Pour over the exposed tail meat. Serve this dish by arranging a central mound of potato salad, top it with salmon caviare, and curl the half lobster around it. Add the dill dressing to the lobster meat, and a pool of Gazpacho Sauce on the other side of the plate.

dishes from left field

Roulade of home-cured mackerel and Bayonne ham, with fresh cod roe sauce (*see opposite*) 128   Pan-fried fish faggots with red pepper coulis 130   Lasagne of sole and spinach in a Stilton béchamel sauce, with leaves, cornichons and capers 132   Meatballs of whole scallops within spicy sausagemeat, coral sauce and shredded mangetout 134   Roast gigot of monkfish and belly pork, with gigandaes plaki 136   'Confit' of shark with celeriac remoulade 138   Salmon with a vanilla pod sauce and a foie gras raviolo 140

Roulade of home-cured mackerel and Bayonne ham, with fresh cod roe sauce

This dish looks most elegant and the Fresh Cod Roe Sauce is particularly fine. Do try and get fresh cod roe: smoked cod roe will do as an alternative, but it is a great deal less subtle. Serves four.

4 fillets Home-cured Mackerel (see page 202)

8 small slices Bayonne ham *or* 4 large ones

2 red onions

250 ml fish stock

150 ml sweetish white wine

50 ml double cream

100 g fresh *or* smoked cod roe

salt and pepper

paprika

juice of 1 lemon

some salad leaves

1 Scrape the cured mackerel from the skin avoiding any dark bits. Chop it finely.

2 Lay out the ham and cover it with the chopped mackerel. Then roll each slice up to make a roulade.

3 To make the sauce, first cook the onions in the stock until the liquid has reduced by two-thirds.

4 Add the wine and reduce by two thirds.

5 Pass through a sieve (or whoosh in a food processor). Then add the cream, and reduce by half.

6 Scrape the roe from its skin while the sauce base cools slightly (you don't want the cod eggs scrambling). Then whisk the roe into the cream mixture. Check the seasoning, which will vary wildly depending on whether you have used fresh or smoked roe, and adjust with salt, pepper, paprika and lemon juice. The sauce should be 'grainy' in the mouth.

Shopping and showing off

Cut each roulade through the middle into two slices and arrange these on the plate with a puddle of sauce. Add some sharp tasting leaves – like rocket – for garnish and contrast. The Fresh Cod Roe Sauce will solidify as it cools so it needs to be warm when served. It's worth making a double quantity of this sauce if you have been lucky enough to get hold of fresh cod roe, as any surplus sauce can be used to make a delicious supper dish. Simply spread a piece of toast with the solidified sauce and pop it under the grill for a minute.

Pan-fried fish faggots

with red pepper coulis

There are two ways of ensuring that these fish faggots hold together: if you have a helpful butcher ask him to let you have some caul fat; if not, use a couple of slices of Parma ham to make neat parcels. The Red Pepper Coulis (see page 199) gives a welcome splash of colour. Makes eight substantial and filling faggots – serves four.

2 red onions

I clove garlic

25 ml olive oil

I fat red chilli

300 g plaice

400 g hake

2 scallops

100 g peeled and deveined Atlantic prawns

2 eggs

½ bunch parsley (½ × 15 g supermarket pack)

4 tablespoons white breadcrumbs

250 g caul fat *or* 16 slices Parma ham

salt and pepper

I quantity Red Pepper Coulis (see page 199)

I Preheat your oven to 200°C/400°F/gas mark 6.

2 Chop the onions and garlic finely and soften in 10 ml of the olive oil with the chilli, which should be chopped finely and seeded if you want to moderate its heat.

3 Skin the plaice and turbot.

4 Take the scallops, prawns, plaice and hake. Mince a third, and chop the other two thirds finely. Beat the eggs, and add them to the fish with the onion mixture, finely chopped parsley and the breadcrumbs. Mix well.

5 Check the seasoning by taking a spoonful of the mix and frying it, then taste and adjust the mixture with salt and pepper.

6 Make up patties with about 120 g of mixture in each. Secure with caul fat – just one layer or the fatty taste will dominate – or make into parcels with two sheets of Parma ham per faggot.

7 Brown off in a frying pan before transferring to the oven for 6–7 minutes.

dishes from left field

Shopping and showing off

Do not use plaice from November to January: they can be very bitter so substitute other white fish. Frozen scallops will do nicely. To serve, float the faggots on a sea of Red Pepper Coulis.

Lasagne of sole and spinach

in a Stilton béchamel sauce, with leaves, cornichons and capers

Complex salads in which every texture and taste plays a part are a feature of many Livebait dishes. Here a spare salad partners a very strange lasagne which sheds a new light on Stilton. Serves four.

125 g butter

60 g flour, plus a little extra

550 ml milk

1 teaspoon nutmeg

1 teaspoon paprika

100 g mature Stilton cheese

200 g Caerphilly

250 g lasagne sheets

1 kg spinach

500 g sole fillets

paprika

salt and pepper

1 bunch flat-leaf parsley (1 × 15 g supermarket pack)

100 g cornichons

50 g caperberries

10 spring onions

1 quantity Balsamic Vinaigrette (see page 193)

1 Preheat your oven to 180°C/350 F/gas mark 4½.

2 Make a béchamel sauce by melting 100 g of the butter in a pan, then adding the flour and cooking it gently. (Ensure that it doesn't turn brown, merely golden.) Heat the milk to just below boiling in another saucepan and whisk it into the flour and butter a ladleful at a time. Add a little grated nutmeg and paprika.

3 Then fold in the cheeses, season to taste, and leave to stand.

4 Precook the lasagne sheets for 5 minutes in boiling salted water, drain and reserve.

5 Wilt the spinach in a minimum amount of boiling salted water for 1 minute and drain.

6 Skin the sole fillets, season, and sear them in a frying pan, with a smear of butter.

7 Butter the lasagne dish and you are ready to assemble. A thin layer of sauce; a layer of lasagne sheets; a layer of sauce; a layer made with half the spinach pressed well down; a layer of lasagne sheets; a layer of sauce; the sole fillets; a layer of lasagne sheets; a layer of sauce; a layer made with the second half of the spinach pressed well down; a layer of lasagne sheets; a layer of sauce.

8 Bake in the oven for 30 minutes. Then brown under the grill if necessary.

9 Prepare the salad by chopping the flat-leaf parsley, the spring onions, quartering the cornichons, and mixing them with the caperberries and a little Balsamic Vinaigrette (see page 193).

Shopping and showing off

If you have trouble finding flat-leafed parsley, use other salad leaves like rocket, frisée or oak-leaf lettuce. The aim is a salad that provides a contrast in both tastes and textures to the rich lasagne. To serve, cut a square portion of lasagne, centre it on the plate and scatter the salad on the surrounds.

Meatballs of whole scallops
within spicy sausagemeat, coral sauce and mangetout

A glass of dry cider goes well with this dish. The end result should be rather like a delicate Scotch egg but with a whole scallop as a surprise centre. One makes a good starter and two a main course. The recipe makes eight.

1 red onion

½ bunch of parsley (½ × 15 g supermarket pack)

1 clove garlic

2 fat red chillies

20 ml light olive oil

1 × 400 g pack of your favourite premium pork sausages

70 ml double cream

nutmeg

8 scallops, with their corals

2 shallots

sweet paprika

200 ml fish stock (see page 186)

200 ml white wine

salt and pepper

300 g mangetout

25 g butter

juice of ½ lemon

1 Preheat your oven to 200°C/400°F/gas mark 6.

2 Chop the onion, parsley, and garlic finely; seed and chop the chillies finely. Soften everything in a frying pan with 10 ml of the olive oil.

3 Rinse the sausages under the tap and you will find the skins slip off easily. Amalgamate the sausagemeat with the onion mixture, add ½ of a grated nutmeg, and 20 ml of the cream.

4 Strip the corals from the scallops and save them. Dry the scallops off carefully with a towel and encase each one in a layer of sausagemeat. Brown well in a frying pan to seal. You need a little practice to keep the balls shut and intact. Press the opening firmly.

5 Transfer to the oven to finish cooking for 5–7 minutes.

6 For the sauce, finely chop the shallots and soften them in the remaining 10 ml of olive

continued overleaf

dishes from left field

oil, add the corals and paprika and cook until everything is beginning to colour.

7 Add the stock and reduce by half.

8 Add the wine and reduce by two thirds.

9 Liquidise with a hand blender (or transfer back and forth to a food processor).

10 Thin the sauce with the remaining cream, adjust the seasoning and keep warm.

11 Top and tail the mangetout and shred them into fine strips with a sharp knife.

12 Cook them quickly in a frying pan with the lemon juice, salt and pepper and the butter.

Shopping and showing off

You can use sausagemeat rather than skinning sausages, but be cautious of the seasoning as commercial sausagemeat can be very salty. To plate up use the contrasting colours of the coral sauce and the mangetout on opposite sides of the meatballs. The Red Pepper Coulis (see page 199) would make a good alternative to the coral sauce.

Roast gigot of monkfish
and belly pork, with gigandaes plaki

A wild combination that is sure to surprise: firm, lean monkfish, smooth, rich belly pork, crisp crackling, melting Greek bean dish. Try this out on the most opinionated of your foodie friends: it will impress them. But remember to start your preparations at least four days in advance so the pork can be properly brined. Serves four.

200 g salt

300 g sugar

4 bay leaves

12 juniper berries

I fat red chilli

I × 750 g piece belly pork, from the meaty end

20 ml runny honey

I × 750 g monkfish tail, skinned and boned

I clove garlic

several branches of rosemary

10 ml olive oil

I quantity Gigandaes Plaki (see page 24)

1 Four days in advance, take a large crock and put in the salt, sugar, bay leaves and juniper berries, also the chilli, chopped finely. Mix well. Add a litre of water and mix well to dissolve the sugar and salt. Add the pork and enough water to ensure that it is covered. Use a plate to keep the joint submerged.

2 Preheat your oven to 200 °C/ 400 °F/gas mark 6.

3 Take the pork out of the brine, and dry it with a towel. It must be very dry for good crackling (at Livebait it gets a blast from a hairdryer to make sure!).

4 Dissolve the honey in 50 ml of the brine liquid and paint over the skin.

5 Roast on a rack for 40 minutes. Then take out and allow to rest while you cook the monkfish.

6 Cut the garlic into slivers and tear the rosemary into sprigs. Make slits all over the monkfish and fill them alternately with garlic and rosemary. Season the fish with salt and pepper and sear it in a frying pan with a minimum of oil.

7 Put in the oven – still at 200°C/400°F/gas mark 6 – for 15–20 minutes.

Shopping and showing off

Make your butcher and fishmonger do their share. Each should be responsible for the preparation work. You need the pork closely scored and the monkfish tail boned out. If the crackling doesn't come out shrapnel crisp you can finish the belly pork with a spell under the grill while the monkfish is roasting. To serve, place a decent helping of Gigandaes Plaki in the centre of a deep plate. Remove the bones from the back of the belly pork and cut the meat into generous slices. Carve similar slices off the monkfish. Arrange a slice of each on top of the plate of beans.

'Confit' of shark

with celeriac remoulade

Very few people have a good word to say about sharks – the *Jaws* movies have a lot to answer for. In the kitchen, however, shark comes into its own – firm, solid meat that takes on other flavours well. At Livebait there is a healthy disdain for convention, and this innovative dish applies the slow cooking technique used to make duck and goose 'confit', to shark ... with fascinating results. Serves four.

500 g goose fat

1 garlic clove

peel of 1 orange

6 juniper berries

12 black peppercorns

1 cinnamon stick

2 bay leaves

500 g piece of shark loin

100 g unsmoked bacon

100 ml red wine

2 tablespoons Worcestershire sauce

1 tablespoon pickled green peppercorns

15 g cold, unsalted butter

salt and pepper

1 quantity Celeriac Remoulade (see page 198)

1 Put the goose fat into a saucepan and add the garlic, finely crushed, orange peel, juniper berries, peppercorns, cinnamon, and bay leaves. Heat up gently to a maximum of 55°C (you need a thermometer, if it gets too hot it will spoil). Cook for an hour.

2 Let the goose fat cool down but do not let it solidify.

3 Portion the shark into 125 g pieces, and pierce with a small knife. Put the shark into the infused goose fat and allow to stand for at least 12 hours in a cool place.

4 Put the pan back on the heat and bring up to 60°C. Cook at this temperature for 20–25 minutes.

5 To make the sauce, dice the bacon finely and fry it gently for 5–6 minutes. Turn the heat up and add the wine and Worcestershire sauce, let it bubble until reduced by half, and then whisk in the cold, cubed butter a little at a time. The sauce will thicken. Add the pickled green peppercorns at the last minute, and adjust the seasoning with salt and pepper.

dishes from left field

Shopping and showing off

Ask your fishmonger for Porbeagle shark loin, including the belly. If this is unavailable, substitute a piece cut from another large, firm fish such as swordfish. The most enjoyable way to secure goose fat is to tuck into a roast goose, but even the French sometimes resort to the tinned goose fat that is available from good food shops. You'll find pickled green peppercorns in small tins at smart shops. To serve, slice the shark portions, arrange them on a mound of Celeriac Remoulade and surround with the red wine sauce.

Salmon with a vanilla pod sauce

and a foie gras raviolo

The very thing to bring out a flair for extravagance. If you cannot think of anywhere that might be able to get in fresh foie gras for you – or merely as a stopgap during the long years when you are saving up to purchase a piece – you can make these ravioli using tinned *bloc de foie gras*. **There's no denying it, fresh foie gras is much nicer.**

2 large fat red chillies

2 mild onions

150 ml Sauternes *or* another sweet white wine

120 g fresh foie gras *or* tinned *bloc de foie gras*

150 g leeks

150 g carrots

150 g celery (preferably the leafy parts)

350 ml white wine

8 black peppercorns

1 bay leaf

juice of 1 lemon

4 × thick 200 g steaks cut from a large salmon

1 quantity simple Pasta Dough (see page 200)

salt and pepper

1 quantity Vanilla Pod Sauce (see page 196–7)

1 Roast the chillies under the grill. Set aside in a sealed plastic bag to cool, then rub off the skins, split and remove the seeds. Chop very finely.

2 Peel and chop the onions very finely.

3 Mix the sweet wine, chillies and chopped onions. Put the foie gras on to a plate and coat thoroughly with the mixture, cover with clingfilm and marinate in a refrigerator for at least 12 hours.

4 Chop the leeks, carrots and celery, and add them to the 350 ml wine, peppercorns, bay leaf and lemon juice in a large pan. Heat until the liquid boils, after 10 minutes turn down to a simmer and lower in the salmon steaks. Poach for 3–5 minutes – they are done if they are resilient when pressed. Skin and put to one side while you cook the ravioli.

5 Divide the pasta dough into four. Then roll it as thinly as you can. Put a quarter of the marinated foie gras and a little of the marinade in a pile, centrally on one half. Season well. Fold the other half of the sheet over. Cut out a circular raviolo about 10 cm across with the foie gras central. Crimp the edges together with a little water.

5 Poach the ravioli in a large pan of salted water that has been brought to the rolling boil. They should take 3–4 minutes. Do them singly or in pairs – they should never be crowded.

Shopping and showing off

If you can buy ready-made fresh ravioli dough, so well and good. To serve, cover the salmon with a good layer of Vanilla Pod Sauce or, if you prefer use the Sauce Choron (see page 195). Add a raviolo to the side of each piece of salmon and pour a little sauce over the fish.

bread

At Livebait we worry about the bread. It may have a strictly supporting role, but if something goes wrong with the day's baking there is no way of getting things back on to an even keel. Customers will be grumpy. The chefs will be at odds with the waiting staff, it guarantees discontent. On the other hand, when crisp-crusted loaves of brightly coloured, delicious-smelling breads are circulating around the dining room you can hear the admiring murmurs, all is right with the world, and the service will go by in a flash.

Yeast is the magic ingredient, both in the making of bread and the brewing of bread's cousin alcohol. Who would have thought that a talent for breathing out CO_2 and the consequent by-products would prove so useful? Bread is made from flour, water, yeast and a little salt, yet as with every superficially simple recipe, once you have grasped the ingredients list your troubles have only just begun. Weighty volumes have been written about bread-making and its mysteries, but few authors have isolated the two key factors.

1 Practice: bread-making is something you teach yourself. If you made a couple of loaves of bread every day, pretty soon you would find that you became good at it. What's more, all the minor adjustments, dos and don'ts, and precautions that take up so much room in the books would soon become second nature. With practice, bread-making is much easier than you think. Persevere. At Livebait we get the constant practice we need.

2 Flexibility: weights, measures, timings, oven heats and so forth are not carved in stone. If you use only a very little yeast to make dough, and then leave it to rise in a cool place, the process may take a lot longer but it will still rise in the end. Similarly, warm the ingredients and everything will happen more quickly. Be flexible about things: there are bound to be some days when you have more time to play with than others; adapt your method to suit. Try things out.

Getting started
A bit of wise shopping can make the whole bread-making process easier.

Flour: at Livebait we use strong, white, organic flour. 'Strong' refers to the amount of gluten in the flour. Strong flours are made from hard grain, which is usually grown in a cold climate. The crusty outside of a French baguette often owes its charm to strong Canadian wheat. We use white flour because we make a lot of coloured breads and they look brighter. We use organic flour from a small supplier because the larger millers use steel roller mills which work much faster than traditional millstones but also generate a lot of heat – heat that can 'cook' the flour a little even before it gets into the bag.

Yeast: live baker's yeast. Thank goodness that some of the large supermarket chains are so keen to convince us of the authenticity of their bakery operations that they will give away fresh yeast to anyone who asks politely! Otherwise it can be bought from traditional bakers. Dried yeast is second best, and if circumstances force you into using it, follow the directions on the packet.

Salt: we use sea salt at Livebait, both within the dough and as a topping. Minute amounts of trace elements make sea salt taste better, and nothing beats it for crunch when sprinkled on a crusty loaf.

Understanding the chemistry

Yeast loves warm, wet and sweet; but is not so keen on the cold or salt! The flour needs physical pummelling to activate the gluten and form a loaf with a good strong structure – the higher the gluten in the flour to begin with the less kneading you have to do.

So all bread-making, however fancy, comes down to a seven-stage plan.

1 Mixing flour, water, salt and yeast thoroughly.
2 Kneading for the gluten.
3 Leaving the dough for the yeast to work and the bread to rise.
4 Knocking back the dough once again, to break up the bubbles made by the yeast and distribute them evenly.
5 Leaving the loaves to rise a second time.
6 Baking.
7 Cooling.

Grasp that and you're ready to bake.

Basic white bread with poppyseeds

At Livebait we always keep back some dough from the previous day to mix with the new batch. This old dough, which has spent the night (or even two or three days – keep it until it smells unreasonably sour) in the refrigerator rising slowly, helps give our bread real character. But, obviously, the first time you bake you do not have any aged dough to hand, so this initial recipe just uses flour. On subsequent baking days replace 10 per cent by weight of the flour with dough. As we are baking in batches we use a large mixer with a dough hook to knead; thankfully, at home you do not have to forgo the pleasure of kneading by hand – it is truly therapeutic.

20 g yeast

1 teaspoon sugar

600 ml water, at blood heat

1.1 kg strong white flour

20 g salt

1 egg

10 g poppyseeds

butter to grease the baking sheet

1 Dissolve the yeast with the sugar in a little of the water, and wait until it is frothy.

2 Mix the flour and salt on a work surface.

3 Make a well in the centre of the heap. Add the rest of the water to the yeast mixture. Draw the flour together by pouring the liquid into the middle, and making a dough by hand.

4 Knead. Remember, you are 'stretching' the gluten within the flour and that is what you should do with the dough. After 7–8 minutes the feel of the dough will change: in some magical way it stops feeling sticky. Whether you are working by hand or with a machine the dough is ready when you spread a little out between your hands and it stretches to a very thin skin without breaking.

5 Oil a bowl and put the dough into it. Cover it with a cloth and put it to rise; inside an airing cupboard the job takes an hour or two; in the refrigerator it may take a day or two.

6 When the dough has doubled in size, return it to the work surface and knead until you have knocked the puffiness out of it.

7 Form it into two long, oval loaves – like miniature versions of those bakery loaves called 'bloomers'. Put them on to a greased baking sheet and set aside to prove for 45 minutes.

8 Preheat your oven to 230°C/450°F/gas mark 8.

9 When they have risen, paint the tops of the loaves with egg wash and sprinkle with poppy seeds. Then make a series of knife cuts across each loaf, on the diagonal and about 1 cm deep.

10 Bake in the oven for 35–40 minutes. Bread is cooked when you can tap the bottom with your finger and it sounds hollow. There is no substitute for experience in judging this; the sooner you start baking regularly the sooner you'll be doing it confidently.

11 When it is cooked, cool on a rack before slicing. Warm bread is delicious, but hot bread is horrid – there has not been a chance for the structure inside to firm up, or for a crust to harden.

bread

Strange breads

When Yannick Tual joined the kitchen at Livebait Covent Garden, he came with a sheaf of French college qualifications. A four-year course in advanced bread-making was one of them, and when he first arrived he was able to state categorically that the fancy breads we serve would be quite impossible to make: the recipes would never work – the resulting loaves would be disastrous. After seeing these brightly coloured, strangely flavoured crusty loaves wolfed down by a steady stream of delighted diners, he has come round to our way of thinking.

The key to inventing new breads is to liquidise whatever you wish to add, then treat the liquid as part of the water content of the dough. Obviously, this strategy works better in some cases than in others but, as with everything to do with bread, experiment until you feel it is working well, then make a note of the particular details for future reference. For the exotic combinations that follow, use the basic bread recipe and adjust as indicated. As you will probably be trying these recipes when you have already made some bread: they include some 'old dough', which should be worked into the new batch with everything else. If you have no old dough simply add another 100 g flour.

Yellow bread – tagine and turmeric

20 g fresh yeast

1 teaspoon sugar

200 ml water

400 ml liquidised Vegetable Tagine (see page 117)

1 kg strong white flour

1 tablespoon ground turmeric

20 g salt

100 g yesterday's dough

1 egg for egg wash

butter to grease the baking sheet

Red bread – chilli jam and paprika

20 g fresh yeast

1 teaspoon sugar

400 ml water

200 ml Chilli Jam (see page 182)

1 kg strong, white flour

1 tablespoon sweet paprika

20 g salt

100 g yesterday's dough

1 egg for egg wash

butter to grease the baking sheet

Green bread – spinach and sultanas

20 g fresh yeast

1 teaspoon sugar

400 ml water

200 g liquidised frozen spinach

1 kg strong white flour

50 g sultanas

20 g salt

100 g yesterday's dough

1 egg for egg wash

butter to grease the baking sheet

Baba ganoush and lemon zest bread

20 g fresh yeast

1 teaspoon sugar

400 ml water

200 ml Baba Ganoush (see page 198)

1 kg strong white flour

zest of 1 lemon

20 g salt

100 g yesterday's dough

1 egg for egg wash

butter to grease the baking sheet

Coconut and stem ginger bread

20 g fresh yeast

1 teaspoon sugar

700 ml water

200 g grated coconut

1 kg strong white flour

70 g stem ginger, chopped finely

20 g salt

100 g yesterday's dough

1 egg for egg wash

butter to grease the baking sheet

Onion and thyme bread

20 g fresh yeast

1 teaspoon sugar

400 ml water

200 g Onion Jam (see page 182)

1 kg strong white flour

1 bunch fresh thyme (1 × 15 g supermarket pack), chopped finely

20 g salt

100 g yesterday's dough

1 egg for egg wash

butter to grease the baking sheet

Sun-dried tomato and mozzarella bread

20 g fresh yeast

1 teaspoon sugar

500 ml water

200 g sun-dried tomatoes, taken from the oil and chopped finely

1 kg strong, white flour

100 g mozzarella, finely diced

20 g salt

100 g yesterday's dough

1 egg for egg wash

butter to grease the baking sheet

Mussel and fennel seed bread

20 g fresh yeast

1 teaspoon sugar

600 ml water

200 g cooked mussels

1 kg strong white flour

1 tablespoon fennel seeds

20 g salt

100 g yesterday's dough

1 egg for egg wash

butter to grease the baking sheet

bread

Fennel and saffron bread

20 g fresh yeast

1 teaspoon sugar

450 ml water

200 g fennel (braised in 200 ml of white wine with $\frac{1}{2}$ g saffron, then liquidised)

1 kg strong white flour

20 g salt

100 g yesterday's dough

1 egg for egg wash

butter to grease the baking sheet

Salt cod and black olive bread

20 g fresh yeast

1 teaspoon sugar

500 ml water

200 g liquidised Brandade Mash (see page 26)

1 kg strong white flour

70 g halved, stoned black olives

10 g salt

100 g yesterday's dough

1 egg for egg wash

butter to grease the baking sheet

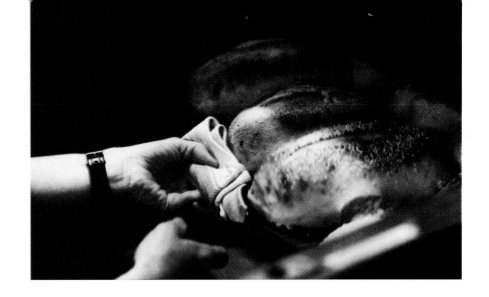

Smoked salmon and green peppercorn bread

20 g fresh yeast

1 teaspoon sugar

600 ml water

100 g smoked salmon cut into long thin strips

1 kg strong white flour

2 tablespoons pickled green peppercorns

10 g salt

100 g yesterday's dough

1 egg for egg wash

butter to grease the baking sheet

Potato bread

20 g yeast

1 teaspoon sugar

500 ml water, at blood heat

550 g strong white flour

550 g plain, well-mashed potato

20 g salt

1 egg

butter to grease the baking sheet

Brioche

This is it then, the ultimate challenge. Very rich, very extravagant, and seriously delicious. There is speculation that when Marie Antoinette said, 'If the poor have no bread, then let them eat cake,' brioche is what she had in mind. Brioche certainly *is* a bread, but only just!

10 g fresh yeast

35 ml warm milk

1 teaspoon salt

350 g strong white flour

6 eggs

150 g unsalted butter

35 g castor sugar

1 Use a food mixer: it will shorten the procedure. Start by beating the yeast and the warm milk slowly with a wire whisk until frothy. Add the salt.

2 Change to a dough hook and, at a slow speed, add the flour and 5 of the eggs.

3 Melt the butter and stir in the sugar.

4 Add the butter mixture a little at a time with the machine running, you should be sure that each lot of mixture is absorbed before adding the next.

5 After about 10 minutes, the mixture should be shiny, elastic and glossy.

6 Transfer to an oiled bowl, cover with a cloth and put in a warm place to prove.

7 When the dough has doubled in size – 1 or 2 hours, depending on how warm its resting place – remove it from the bowl and flip it lightly with your fingers to 'knock it back'.

8 Return it to the bowl and put it into the refrigerator for several hours to rest (but no longer than 24 hours).

9 To bake, preheat your oven to 230°C/450°F/gas mark 8. A saucepan with an ovenproof handle makes a fine stand-in brioche mould, so take one that's about 20 cm in diameter and line it with a large sheet of greased baking parchment being sure that it comes up above the rim. Work your dough into a suitably sized ball and put it into the saucepan.

10 Take the remaining egg and paint the top of the brioche with its yolk. Don't let the glaze run into any cracks in the dough, or 'glue' the sides of the brioche to the pan or paper, as this will inhibit the final rising. Put the pan in a warm place while the brioche rises. Once again it will nearly double its bulk.

11 Bake immediately for 40–45 minutes.

12 When cooked, remove from the saucepan and cool on a wire rack.

sweets

Chocolate and orange cake

with vanilla sauce

This is a chocolate layer cake which is made using a large patisserie ring at Livebait. In the home kitchen it is easier to assemble it in a deep-sided 20-cm cake tin. This cake will make six good slices.

6 eggs, separated

310 g castor sugar

60 g cornflour

60 g flour

80 g cocoa

125 ml whipping cream

125 ml milk

250 ml freshly squeezed orange juice

50 g glucose

750 g dark cooking chocolate (70% cocoa solids)

1 quantity Vanilla Sauce (see page 177)

1 Preheat your oven to 220°C/425°F/gas mark 7.

2 Whisk the egg yolks with 120 g of the sugar until the mixture is fluffy and looks 'white'.

3 In another bowl whisk the egg whites, gradually add 40 g of sugar, and whisk until they hold a firm peak.

4 Put the cornflour, flour and 30 g of the cocoa into a sieve and work them gradually into the egg-yolk mixture.

5 Then fold the combination of flour, sugar and yolks into the egg whites.

6 Divide the mixture into 3 and cook in 20-cm sponge tins. Spread the mixture out with a palette knife.

7 Bake for 15–20 minutes. Remove from the oven and put flat on a work surface to cool.

8 To make the cocoa syrup, dissolve the remaining 150 g of sugar in 125 ml water and add 30 g of the cocoa. Stir to mix thoroughly and cool.

9 To make the orange chocolate ganache, bring the whipping cream and the milk, the orange juice and the glucose up to the boil, and take off the heat.

10 Melt the chocolate in a bowl over boiling water, then steadily whisk the hot orange cream into the chocolate.

11 To assemble the cake, take a 20-cm spring-sided cake tin and use it as a mould for the 3 discs of cake. Place the first one in the bottom of the tin and brush liberally with the cocoa syrup.

12 To make the next layer, use half the orange chocolate ganache, evenly spread with a palette knife.

13 Then another layer of cake brushed with syrup.

14 Then the rest of the ganache.

15 Brush the underside of the last piece of cake with syrup and add it.

16 Put the whole into the refrigerator for 30 minutes to set.

Shopping and showing off

If you cannot obtain glucose, use a similar weight of sugar. To serve, sieve a little cocoa powder on to the top of the cake before slicing; surround each slice with Vanilla Sauce.

Almond pithiviers

with bitter chocolate sauce

The best Pithiviers are made from a tightly layered butter puff pastry. One of the patissiers at Livebait, Yannick Tual, used to work for Monsieur Gouin Régis of Mortagne au Perche. The same Monsieur Gouin Régis who regularly won the annual Pithiviers competition held in the town of that name. The Livebait Pithiviers is the real thing – melting pastry and with a rich heart. If you would rather substitute bought ready-made butter puff pastry, it will still be delicious, but Regis Gouin would certainly raise an eyebrow. Makes a Pithiviers about 24 cm in diameter. Serves eight.

450 g flour

5 g salt

450 g butter

8 tablespoons water

3 eggs

200 g castor sugar

200 g ground almonds

1 quantity Bitter Chocolate Sauce (see page 177)

1 Take the 250 g of flour, and the salt. Rub in 25 g of the butter with your fingertips. Make it into pastry with the water. Wrap it in clingfilm and rest it in the refrigerator for 2–3 hours.

2 Take 225 g of the butter – cold from the refrigerator. Place it on a board and hit it with your rolling pin until it is malleable but still cold and firm. Level it out so that you have a flat piece of butter.

3 Flour the work surface and roll out the pastry into a rough square. Then roll each side until it makes a broad cross. Put the cold butter into the centre of the cross and fold in the arms to enclose the butter. Put the whole thing back in the refrigerator for 30 minutes.

4 Put the pastry on to a floured work surface with the 'joins' underneath and gently roll it out into a rectangle three times as long as it is wide, and about 5 mm thick.

5 Fold the left third into the middle, and do the same with the right third. Take the square you now have and roll it out into a rectangle once more, working away from you.

6 When you have a rectangle again, fold each half in as before to make a square. Scratch an arrow on it lightly to show the direction of the last rolling. Wrap it up and rest it in the refrigerator.

continued overleaf

7 Repeat steps 5 and 6 rolling it out at right angles to the previous direction.

8 Repeat steps 5 and 6 rolling it out at right angles to the previous direction. Congratulations, you have butter puff pastry!

9 Preheat your oven to 200°C/400°F/gas mark 6.

10 Beat the eggs in a bowl.

11 Make the almond filling by creaming together 200 g of butter and 200 g of sugar, work in the ground almonds and half the egg. Reserve the other half of the egg for egg wash.

12 Take half the pastry and roll it out. Use a suitable saucepan lid to mark out a circle about 24 cm in diameter.

13 Spread the filling carefully in the centre of the circle, it should be 15 mm thick and there should be a 3-cm border all the way around the edge.

14 Roll out the other half of the pastry as a lid and press the border down hard. You should end up with something that looks very much like a flattened cardinal's hat.

15 Put the Pithiviers on to a parchment-lined baking sheet, make a central steam vent. Transfer to the refrigerator for at least an hour.

16 Before baking, brush with the remaining egg. Then decorate (see the photographs opposite).

17 Bake for about 30 minutes, then lift an edge carefully from the paper with a palette knife; the Pithiviers is done if it is nicely browned and crisp.

Shopping and showing off

This is a difficult dish so ready-made pastry is fair enough, but not so delicious. You can make it the day before and leave it in the refrigerator overnight for its final 'rest' before baking. Serve with a fanfare of boastful trumpets and some of the excellent (and very easy) Bitter Chocolate Sauce.

Lime mousse and craquelin

The craquelin makes this a very pretty dish. Like a sugary biscuit, but thin and elegant, at Livebait the craquelin is used like a tuile biscuit to provide the sail for a raft of mousse. Makes a big bowl of mousse, serves at least eight.

20 g lime zest (10 limes)

4 leaves gelatine *or* 2 sachets gelatine powder

juice of 10 limes

pulp of 3 limes

600 g castor sugar

1 litre whipping cream

10 g flour

100 g butter

100 g flaked almonds

1 Put the lime zest into cold water, bring to the boil. Sieve the zest and repeat three times. This will remove any bitterness from the lime peel.

2 Soften the gelatine sheets in a little lime juice.

3 Warm half the remaining lime juice, with half the zest, and the pulp in a saucepan with 200 g of the sugar, stirring until it is dissolved.

4 Add the softened gelatine and stir until dissolved, allow to cool.

5 Whip the cream until it is stiff, then fold in the lime-juice mixture.

6 Transfer to a bowl and allow to set in the refrigerator overnight.

7 To make the craquelin, preheat your oven to 200°C/400°F/gas mark 6.

8 Sift the flour and the remaining 400 g of sugar together.

9 Melt the butter and add, with the remaining lime juice and zest, to the flour and sugar. Chop the almonds finely, then add them. Mix with your fingers until you have a gritty texture like coarse, wet sand.

10 Line a baking tray with baking parchment. Make small piles of the craquelin mixture – about the size of a walnut. They must be well spaced as they will liquefy in the oven's heat and spread out like biscuits.

11 Bake for 5–7 minutes. They are cooked when they are transparent in the middle and dark around the edges.

12 When they are done remove the tray from the oven and lift off the paper with the craquelin on it, putting it directly on to a work surface to cool quickly.

Nougat glacé Créole

This is an extremely delicious pudding that neatly balances textures and tastes. Prepare it in advance, then simply slice and serve. The only special equipment you will need is a thermometer – getting the temperature right is the key to ending up with the right texture – so it's time to retrieve that jam thermometer languishing at the back of your cupboard, and put it to work. Makes enough to fill a 2-litre ice-cream carton.

100 g currants

50 ml dark rum

180 g castor sugar

50 g flaked almonds

3 egg whites

100 g honey

500 ml whipping cream

seasonal fruit for coulis

1 At least 24 hours before you start cooking put the currants to soak in the rum.

2 You also need to pre-prepare the nougatine. Take 100 g of the sugar, put it in a dry pan. Heat it until it melts, and then continue until it is a nice golden brown. Watch it closely as it turns black and bitter in what seems like the twinkling of an eye.

3 Stir the flaked almonds into the liquid sugar and pour on to a baking sheet lined with baking parchment. Allow to cool. When completely cold, break into small pieces with rolling pin, or use a food processor – you are aiming for small chunks not dust!

4 Put the egg whites into your food processor or blender, but do not start it yet.

5 Put the honey, the remaining 80 g of sugar and 50 ml of water into a pan and boil until the temperature reaches 112°C. Use your jam thermometer and try to be precise. When the syrup reaches that temperature, turn the heat down very low.

6 Start your food processor and whoosh until the egg whites form soft peaks. Turn it off.

7 Back to the stove, turn the heat up and wait until your thermometer reads 121°C. You must not allow your syrup to get hotter than this or it will burn.

8 Turn the food processor back on. Gradually pour the hot syrup on to the beaten egg whites while the processor is running. The two should mix together and produce a glossy Italian meringue mixture that is just as stiff as the egg whites were before you added the syrup. Turn into a large bowl and allow to cool.

9 Whip the cream until stiff – it should just form a peak.

10 Fold the cream, the currants, and the nougatine into the meringue.

11 Put all the mix into a large terrine dish, or a plastic ice-cream container, and leave in the freezer for at least 12 hours.

Shopping and showing off

The Nougat glacé Créole is 'soft scoop' and can be served straight from the freezer. Cut slices with a serrated knife that has been dipped in hot water. To dress the plate, make a simple coulis from seasonal fruits – anything with enough acidity to give sharpness. Take 200 g of fruit and purée in a liquidiser or food processor, sieve to remove any pips and adjust the taste to suit with sugar and lemon juice.

Banana tart with lemon granita

The slight crunch of the Lemon granita goes terribly well with the richness of the Banana Tart. At Livebait, individual tarts are the rule, but there's no reason why you shouldn't make a single large one. This quantity makes a 24-cm tart and a 1-litre ice-cream carton of Granita. Serves six to eight.

25 g lemon zest

150 ml lemon juice (4–6 lemons)

375 ml water

125 g sugar

50 g glucose

175 g butter

175 g castor sugar

1 egg

350 g flour

6 ripe bananas

100 g ground almonds

2 egg yolks

1 First make the lemon granita. Put the lemon zest into cold water and bring to the boil. Strain the zest and repeat three times. This will remove any bitterness from the peel.

2 Warm the water, lemon juice, water, sugar and glucose in a pan. If you cannot get glucose use 100 g more sugar.

3 When all is dissolved stir in the lemon zest, pour into an ice-cream carton and place in the coldest part of your freezer.

4 Remove after 60 minutes and stir vigorously with a fork to break up any crystals. Put back in the freezer.

5 Repeat after another 30 minutes

6 And once more, after another 30 minutes.

7 When you want to serve the granita, simply move it from the freezer to the refrigerator 30 minutes before you want it, and stir well before serving. It should have the texture of a 'Slush Puppy'.

For the tart

1 Beat 75 g of the butter and 75 g of the sugar together in a bowl.

2 Beat the egg and work it in with a fork (saving a tiny amount to use as egg wash later).

3 Add 350 g of the flour and pull together into pastry initially with a fork and then with your hands. Keep everything cool and light! Wrap the pastry in clingfilm and put into the refrigerator to rest for at least 60 minutes.

4 Preheat your oven to 200°C/400°F/gas mark 6.

5 Roll out the pastry until it is 3 mm thick. Line a 20-cm flan tin or 6 individual flan cases.

6 Bake blind (put some parchment and a layer of beans in the tart to keep the pastry flat) for 10 minutes.

7 Remove the beans and brush the inside of the tart with a little egg wash and return to the oven for a further 3 minutes.

8 Cut the bananas into slices about 1 cm long, and arrange them ends down, so that they fill the pastry case.

9 Turn the oven down to 180°C/350°F/gas mark $4\frac{1}{2}$, put in the tart until the banana is cooked – about 10 minutes.

10 Make the sablé topping. Use your fingertips to rub together the butter, sugar, ground almonds, and the egg yolks. The mixture should end up 'gritty' and feel a bit like damp sand.

11 Sprinkle the topping over the tarts until the bananas are completely covered and you have a nice flat surface. Turn the oven up to 200°C/400°F/gas mark 6, and bake until golden brown – about 10 minutes.

Shopping and showing off

If there is no glucose in the cake-making section at the supermarket, you can usually find it at the chemist. Serve the tart with the granita served separately in a ramekin.

Chestnut and whisky mousse cake

Making it into a mousse goes some way towards taming the incredible richness of chestnut purée. At Livebait we make individual mousses, but in the home it's easier to make a single cake. Use a 20-cm diameter, high-sided cake tin and you will have enough for eight slices.

5 eggs

275 g castor sugar

125 g melted butter

125 g strong white flour

125 ml water

250 g tinned 'crème de marrons' (sweet)

250 g tinned 'chestnut purée' (unsweetened)

5 gelatine leaves *or* 2 sachets gelatine powder

500 ml whipping cream

75 ml whisky

15 g cocoa powder

I Preheat your oven to 220°C/425°F/gas mark 7.

2 Whisk the eggs with 125 g of the sugar very well – until the mix sticks to the end of your finger. Drizzle in the melted butter and continue to beat.

3 Sieve the flour slowly into the egg mixture, mixing as you go. You should end up with a mixture that resembles a very liquid mousse.

4 Line a baking sheet with baking parchment and use a palette knife to spread the mixture out into a layer about 1 cm thick.

5 Bake in the oven until golden brown – 8–10 minutes. Remove and lift the parchment and cake off the baking tray, put it down on a cold work surface to cool. This will help stop it drying out.

6 Line a 20-cm high-sided cake tin with a tall funnel of baking parchment.

7 Mix the two chestnut purées together very well in a large bowl.

8 Soften the gelatine sheets in a little water.

9 Bring 50 ml of the whipping cream up to the boil, take off the heat and stir in the softened gelatine sheets. Add 50 ml of the whisky and mix into the chestnut puree.

10 Whip the remaining 450 ml of cream until it forms soft peaks.

11 Fold it into the chestnut mixture a little at a time.

12 Take the remaining 25 ml of whisky and warm it with the remaining 150 g of sugar until you have a syrup.

13 Cut a circle of cake that fits exactly and put it into the lined tin. Brush with the whisky syrup.

14 Fill up with the chestnut mousse, banging the tin down gently to settle the mixture and drive out air-pockets. Put into the refrigerator until set – about 12 hours.

15 To serve remove from the tin, dust the top of the cake with a little cocoa and slice.

Shopping and showing off

Most supermarkets stock a surprisingly sophisticated range of chestnut products – look out for the name Clément Faugier. The crème de marrons is very sweet, the purée less so. If you can only obtain the purée, use it as a substitute for the crème and add 50 g of sugar and a few drops of vanilla essence. This dessert needs nothing more adding than a little double cream.

Chocolate and pear tart

You can just as easily make individual portions of this very rich tart as one large one. And if you feel an extravagant impulse coming on, you can flambé the pears in a glass of brandy rather than poaching them in syrup – bearing in mind that when you choose this route you should buy slightly riper fruit. Makes a 24-cm diameter tart. Serves six.

150 g butter

300 g castor sugar

1 egg

300 g flour

350 ml water

1 vanilla pod

4 pears

250 ml whipping cream

250 g honey

250 g good quality dark chocolate

125 g milk chocolate

1 Beat the 150 g of butter and 150 g of the sugar together in a bowl.

2 Work in the egg with a fork (saving a tiny amount to use as egg wash later).

3 Add the flour and pull together into pastry with a fork and then your hands. Keep everything cool and light! Wrap the pastry in clingfilm and put into the refrigerator to rest for at least 60 minutes. Take out and bring back to room temperature before rolling.

4 Preheat your oven to 200°C/400°F/gas mark 6.

5 Roll out the pastry until it is 3 mm thick. Use it to line a 24-cm diameter flan tin.

6 Bake blind (put some parchment and a layer of beans in the tart to keep the pastry flat) for 20 minutes.

7 Remove the beans and brush the inside of the tart with a little egg wash, return to the oven for a further 5 minutes.

8 Meanwhile, make up a syrup by dissolving 150 g of sugar in 350 ml of water and adding a vanilla pod split lengthways.

9 Peel, halve and core the pears and cook them in the syrup until soft. Drain and slice into pieces less than 1 cm thick.

10 Bring the whipping cream and honey to the boil. Remove from the heat.

11 Melt the two chocolates in a bowl over hot water, then add them to the hot cream and honey. Stir the mixture thoroughly.

12 Arrange the pear slices in the tart case, pour over the chocolate until the pears are completely submerged and you have a smooth surface. Cool until set.

Shopping and showing off

The dark chocolate should be 70 per cent cocoa solids. Serve this tart alone in all its glory as it is extremely rich – the possible exception being to consider adding a dollop of clotted cream on the edge of the plate.

Bitter chocolate sauce

So easy. So good ! Makes approximately 500 ml.

250 ml milk

150 g dark chocolate (70 per cent cocoa solids)

80 ml whipping cream

40 g unsalted butter

1 Heat the milk until boiling in a saucepan.

2 Whisk in the chocolate.

3 Whisk in the cream.

4 Whisk in the butter.

Sweet vanilla sauce

This is a sophisticated kind of custard, but custard nevertheless! Makes approximately 900 ml.

500 ml milk

2 vanilla pods

6 egg yolks

200 g sugar

100 ml whipping cream

1 Put the milk into a saucepan. Split the vanilla pods lengthways and strip the seeds into the milk, then add the pods. Bring to the boil and turn off immediately.

2 Whisk the egg yolks and sugar until they are fluffy and look 'white'.

3 Whip the cream.

4 Remove the vanilla pods from the milk with a straining spoon.

5 Put the egg yolk mixture into a saucepan and, over a minimal heat, steadily whisk in the hot milk. As the sauce starts to thicken remove the pan from the heat and whisk in the whipped cream.

Shopping and Showing off

This sauce should be light and frothy and benefits from being served no hotter than lukewarm.

pickles, preserves and sauces

Tomato chutney

This is a stunning red chutney, which needs to be made from really ripe tomatoes. As tomatoes are so often only half ripe when you buy them, remember to get them a few days in advance and allow them to ripen fully before you start. Makes approximately 1.5 kg of chutney.

150 g root ginger

450 g cooking apples

300 g Spanish onions

1.5 kg ripe tomatoes

225 g sultanas

225 g Demerara sugar

1 dessertspoon salt

450 ml malt vinegar

1 teaspoon cayenne pepper

2 teaspoons mustard powder

1 Peel the root ginger, cut it into 3 cm lengths, bruise them with a hammer. Then tie them up in a piece of muslin.

2 Peel, core and chop the apples very finely. Skin and chop the onions very finely. Skin the tomatoes and chop them roughly.

3 Put all the ingredients and the muslin-bagged ginger into a large non-reactive saucepan. Bring to the boil, then reduce the heat and simmer gently, uncovered, for about two hours. Stir occasionally.

4 The chutney is ready when it is thick, has an even consistency and there is no longer any excess liquid.

5 Remove the muslin-wrapped ginger and spoon the chutney into sterilised jars. Cover immediately with airtight and vinegar-proof tops. It will be ready to eat after three weeks and will keep for up to three months. Refrigerate after opening.

pickles, preserves and sauces

Chermoula

One of the basic building blocks of taste, providing a complex base flavour for a variety of dishes. Make this up fresh, as and when you need it, to retain the colour and pungency. Makes approximately 250ml of paste.

2 Spanish onions

3 cloves garlic

1 bunch flat-leafed parsley (1 × 15 g supermarket pack)

1½ bunches fresh coriander leaves (2 × 15 g supermarket pack)

2 dessertspoons chilli powder

2 dessertspoons cumin powder

2 dessertspoons turmeric powder

2 dessertspoons sweet paprika

25 ml salt

50 ml olive oil

juice of 1 lemon

1 Chop the onions and garlic roughly.

2 Put them and the remaining ingredients into a food processor or liquidiser and whoosh until you have a fine paste.

Chilli jam

Makes approximately 750 ml of jam.

4 red onions

2 red peppers

light olive oil

20 small hot chillies

2 punnets cherry tomatoes

100 g palm sugar *or* muscovado sugar

150 ml Thai fish sauce (nam plah)

1 Chop the onions and red peppers finely. Put in a pan and barely cover with olive oil.

2 Chop the chillies and add them. Fry until all is golden brown.

3 Chop the tomatoes in half, then add, and carry on cooking until all is dark brown.

4 Add the sugar and fish sauce and whoosh in a food processor or liquidiser.

Red onion jam

Makes approximately 500 ml of jam.

500 g red onions

1 clove garlic

2 fat red chillies

100 g butter

20 ml balsamic vinegar

1 Chop the onions and garlic finely. Seed and chop the chillies finely. Sweat them all in the butter. Cook slowly, with the lid on, for an hour.

2 Stir in the balsamic vinegar and use when cold. Do not keep for more than a couple of days.

Tapenade

Makes approximately 300 g of tapenade.

100 g stoned black olives

100 g caperberries, without their stalks

100 g tin anchovy fillets in oil

$\frac{1}{2}$ fat red chilli

6 sprigs fresh rosemary

1 Put the olives, caperberries, and anchovies (plus the oil from the tin) into a blender or food-processor. Seed the chilli, chop it finely, and add that. Strip the leaves from the rosemary stalks and add them.

2 Whoosh everything together until well chopped and mixed, but still fairly chunky. Beware of going too far – you'd end up with a formless mush.

Szechuan pickled cucumbers
and black shiitake mushrooms

This pickle provides both contrasting textures and a pleasant tang – some would call it fiery, so if you don't warm to chilli heat remove the chillies after they have been fried. Makes approximately 300 ml of pickle.

25 dried shiitake mushrooms

500 g cucumber

salt

250 ml groundnut oil

2 tablespoons Szechuan peppercorns

10 small hot chillies

100 g root ginger

100 g white sugar

50 ml light soy sauce

50 ml of rice vinegar

1 Put the mushrooms into a bowl of warm water to rehydrate.

2 Peel and seed the cucumbers, cut them into batons diagonally and lengthways. Salt lightly for 30 minutes to draw out the water.

3 Bring the oil to smoking point in a wok or large frying pan, add the peppercorns and wait until they turn black, then remove with a straining spoon.

4 Reheat the oil and add the chillies, when they go black add the ginger, peeled and shredded finely. It will spit and splutter a good deal.

5 Add the white sugar, soy sauce and rice vinegar, plus the cucumber batons and mushrooms – pat them dry with a kitchen towel first.

6 Stir around for a minute or two to amalgamate the flavours, then transfer to a bowl. Leave for a day or two to mature.

Apple and sultana chutney

Makes approximately 1.5 kg of chutney.

500 g cooking apples

30 g galangal

30 g stem ginger

150 g macadamia nuts

2 fat red chillies

500 g sultanas

2 cloves garlic

1 tablespoon sweet paprika

350 g granulated sugar

1 tablespoon cayenne pepper

2 cloves

1 tablespoon celery salt

400 ml cider vinegar

100 ml mirin – sweet cooking saké

1 Peel and core the apples, then chop them finely. Peel and chop the galangal finely. Chop the stem ginger. Roast and chop the macadamia nuts finely. Seed and chop the chillies finely. Mix with the other ingredients thoroughly, cover with clingfilm and leave in a cool place for 4–5 hours, stirring the mixture occasionally. Pack into jars and seal well. Mature for a month before use.

Fish stock

Makes approximately 2 litres.

250 g carrots

1 head celery

250 g leeks

250 g onions

1 head of garlic

1 kg fish trimmings: best are sole trimmings; then any flatfish trimmings; also monkfish bones; heads are
good but every trace of gills must be removed – blood is the enemy of good fish stock

1 bottle white wine – not your best

5 bay leaves

several sprigs each of fresh tarragon, dill and parsley

12 black peppercorns

1 Peel the carrots, then chop them roughly with the rest of the unpeeled vegetables. Cut the unpeeled garlic into 2 pieces horizontally. Put them all in a large pot, add the wine, the fish, herbs and enough water to barely cover everything.

2 Bring to the boil, and boil for 10 minutes, skimming off the impurities.

3 Reduce the temperature to a simmer and continue to cook for 40 minutes, skimming occasionally.

4 If your stock is destined for soup, pass it through a sieve and reduce by half to concentrate the flavour.

5 If it is to be used in a sauce, pass through a sieve and use as it is.

Chicken stock

Makes approximately 2 litres of stock.

250 g carrots

1 head celery

250 g leeks

250 g onions

1 head of garlic

2 chicken carcasses *or* the equivalent in bits and pieces – chicken wings are often the cheapest option

1 bottle white wine – not your best!

5 bay leaves

several sprigs fresh parsley

12 black peppercorns

1 tablespoon sweet paprika

1 Peel the carrots, then chop them roughly with the rest of the unpeeled veg. Slice the unpeeled garlic head in half horizontally. Put everything into a large pot and just cover with water.

2 Bring to the boil for 10 minutes, skimming off the impurities.

3 Reduce the temperature to a simmer and continue to cook for 50 minutes, skimming continually.

4 Pass through a sieve and reduce by a third before use.

Vegetable stock

The Livebait recipe for vegetable stock reflects the fact that there is always an amazing range of fresh vegetables to hand. If you have the time (and the inclination), make this stock according to the recipe at least once – it's interesting to see what an intense and fresh flavour it delivers. Then, when you need a vegetable stock in the future, use it as a starting point and omit any three or four of the components that are unavailable. Makes approximately 2 litres of stock.

3 leeks

3 carrots

2 stalks celery

2 red onions

I head garlic

3 plum tomatoes

I parsnip

I turnip

I bunch flat parsley (2 × 15 g supermarket packs)

$\frac{1}{2}$ bunch rosemary (I × 15 g supermarket pack)

$\frac{1}{2}$ bunch thyme (I × 15 g supermarket pack)

$\frac{1}{2}$ bunch oregano (I × 15 g supermarket pack)

$\frac{1}{2}$ bunch chervil (I × 15 g supermarket pack)

3 bay leaves

6 black peppercorns

2.5 litres tap water

1 Clean and chop the leeks, celery, and onions, leaving the skin on. Peel and chop the carrots. Cut the garlic head in half horizontally. Seed and halve the plum tomatoes. Scrub and chop the root vegetables. Chop the herbs roughly.

2 Put everything into a large pan with the water, bring to the boil, reduce the heat and simmer for 90 minutes.

3 Strain off the stock through a sieve, pressing the vegetable residue with a spoon to squeeze out all the juices.

Aïoli

If you want it a touch more pungent you can add further garlic. It is still the advice of the government that we do not eat raw eggs, which rules out Aïoli unless your supermarket stocks those prepacked, pasteurised egg yolks. If you disagree with the official line and wish to take the responsibility on yourself, use really good fresh eggs that are free range and come from a flock certified free of salmonella. Makes about 300 ml of Aïoli.

4 cloves garlic

salt and black pepper

I egg yolk

250 ml good olive oil

Using a mortar and pestle

Working by hand

I With a pestle and mortar pound the garlic in the mortar with a good pinch of salt and some pepper.

2 Add the egg yolk and work in.

3 Add the oil gradually until you have a thick emulsion – like mayonnaise.

4 Adjust the seasoning with salt and pepper.

Using a blender or food processor

I Put in everything but the oil, and whoosh together.

2 Leave the machine running as you trickle the oil in to produce a thick emulsion.

3 Adjust the seasoning with salt and pepper.

Horseradish cream

This will put you off shop-bought horseradish sauce for ever. Although nothing is quite like freshly grated horseradish root, the next best thing is the commercial grated horseradish that you sometimes find in jars at smart food shops. Makes approximately 300 ml.

200 g fresh horseradish root

200 ml crème fraîche

1 squeeze of lemon juice

10 ml spoon salt

1 Peel the horseradish root with a potato peeler, then grate it into a bowl using the fine side of your grater. Do not inhale deeply – horseradish is fiercely pungent.

2 Add the lemon juice and salt, mix thoroughly. Then add a little crème fraîche and mix in. Continue adding a bit at a time until there's just enough cream to bind the mixture. Treat the project as if you were making coleslaw in miniature.

Foie gras vinaigrette

Makes approximately 220 ml of vinaigrette.

100 g fresh foie gras *or* tinned *bloc de foie gras*

100 ml light olive oil

50 ml balsamic vinegar

6 caperberries

1 Put the foie gras into a cocotte dish and stand it in a pan of boiling water, until it has just firmed up. Take off the stove and allow to cool.

2 Put it with the other ingredients in a food processor and whizz until all is liquid.

3 Enjoy the self-indulgence, and the richness!

Balsamic vinaigrette

Makes approximately 220 ml.

3 tablespoons grain mustard

2 tablespoons honey

100 ml balsamic vinegar

100 ml extra virgin olive oil

salt and pepper to taste

▌ Mix together thoroughly by shaking in a screw-topped jar.

Harissa vinaigrette

Makes approximately 220 ml.

3 tablespoons grain mustard

1 tablespoon Harissa paste

2 tablespoons honey

100 ml red wine vinegar

100 ml extra virgin olive oil

salt to taste

▌ Mix together thoroughly, by shaking in a screw-topped jar. Beware – hot!

Pernod sauce

An amazing sauce. So simple. So delicious. So try it! Makes approximately 150 ml of sauce.

150 ml Pernod

50 g cold butter

salt and pepper

1 Take a stainless steel pan and heat it up, pour in the Pernod and allow to bubble.
2 Cut the butter (which must be chilled – straight from the refrigerator) into small cubes.
3 When the Pernod has reduced by a third, whisk in the butter a little at a time. The sauce will thicken and 'polish' up, becoming glossy.
4 Taste the sauce and adjust the seasoning.

Sauce gribiche

Makes approximately 200 ml of sauce.

100 ml olive oil

20 ml red wine vinegar

50 ml smooth Dijon mustard

2 hard-boiled eggs

50 g cornichons

50 g small caperberries

salt and pepper

1 Mix the oil and vinegar in a bowl, and stir in the mustard.
2 Finely chop the hard-boiled eggs and add them. Roughly chop the cornichons and add them.
3 Stir in the caperberries, then adjust the seasoning.

Sauce choron

Makes approximately 200 ml of sauce.

2 shallots

150 ml white wine

50 ml tarragon vinegar

1 tablespoon fresh tarragon

8 peppercorns

3 egg yolks

1 tablespoon strong English mustard powder

1 tablespoon tomato purée

25 g soft butter

175 g melted butter

salt

juice of $\frac{1}{2}$ lemon

1 plum tomato

1 Chop the shallots very finely and put them with the wine, tarragon vinegar, fresh tarragon and peppercorns into a pan and heat until bubbling. Cook until reduced by a third.

2 Whisk the egg yolks and mustard in a large bowl – the right size to sit easily over a saucepan of hot water during the next stage.

3 Stir the tomato purée into the vinegar mixture, allow to cool and strain through a fine sieve on to the egg yolks.

4 Take a whisk and beat the egg-yolk mixture over a pan of hot water. (You seek to keep the sauce warm but never too hot or the eggs will scramble.) It will help if you start by whisking in a little (25 ml) lukewarm water. Then whisk in the soft butter a little at a time until the sauce is thick and glossy.

5 Now add the melted butter – a little at a time – whisking as you go. Finally, season with salt and lemon juice to taste. Peel, seed, and dice the tomato finely; stir it in. Keep the sauce warm over hot water until required.

Gazpacho sauce

Makes approximately 200 ml of sauce.

5 large plum tomatoes

I clove garlic

I small red onion

3 tablespoons breadcrumbs

30 ml good olive oil

10 ml sherry vinegar

salt and pepper

1 Preheat your oven to 200°C/400°F/gas mark 6.

2 Cut the tomatoes in half and roast on a baking tray in the oven for 15 minutes.

3 Peel and chop the garlic and onion, and place them with the other ingredients in a blender and whoosh until liquidised.

4 Pass the sauce through a sieve.

5 Adjust seasoning.

Vanilla pod sauce

Makes approximately 150 ml.

6 vanilla pods

2 shallots

200 ml white wine

150 ml water

juice of $\frac{1}{2}$ lemon

80 ml double cream

zest I lemon

1 Split the vanilla pods lengthways and strip the tiny seeds into a pan.

2 Add the pods, shallots, wine, water and lemon juice.

3 Heat until bubbling, then cook until reduced by two thirds.

4 Remove from the heat and leave to infuse for 10 minutes, then remove the pieces of vanilla pod and whisk in the cream and lemon zest. Warm through gently, but do not allow to boil or the sauce will split.

5 Season with a little salt.

Cumin sauce

Makes approximately 150 ml of sauce.

2 teaspoons cumin seeds

2 Spanish onions

1 clove garlic

20 ml olive oil

300 ml fish stock (see page 186)

300 ml white wine

100 g cold, unsalted butter

salt and pepper

1 Toast the cumin seeds in a dry pan, and reserve.

2 Finely chop the onions; peel and crush the garlic. Soften them both in a little oil in a frying pan.

3 Add the cumin and the fish stock, then reduce by half.

4 Add the wine and reduce by two-thirds so that you end up with 150 ml of liquid.

5 Pass through a sieve into a clean pan, bring to the boil and whisk in the chilled butter straight from the fridge, cut into cubes, a little at a time – this will give a glossy, thickened sauce. Adjust seasoning to taste.

Celeriac remoulade

If you make the sauce first, then grate the celeriac into it, you avoid having to keep the celeriac in acidulated water to avoid it blackening. Makes approximately 500 g.

150 g crème fraîche

2 tablespoons Dijon mustard

juice of 1 lemon

2 tablespoons pickled green peppercorns

salt

300 g celeriac root

sweet paprika

1 Mix the crème fraîche with the mustard and lemon juice, stir in the peppercorns and season to taste with salt.

2 Peel the celeriac and shred it as finely as you are able; as you go, fold it into the crème fraîche mixture.

3 When serving, sprinkle a pinch of paprika over the top.

Baba ganoush

This aubergine 'paste', is a good source of taste and an instant marinade – very useful. Makes approximately 300 ml.

2 large aubergines

2 cloves garlic

30 ml tahini paste

juice of $\frac{1}{2}$ lemon

1 tablespoon cumin powder

salt to taste

1 Cook the aubergines under a grill, or by turning them over a naked flame on a fork until they are black, then place them in a plastic bag and put to one side.

2 When they are cold simply rub off the skins with your fingers, peeling any stubborn patches with a knife. Squeeze out the bitter juices – again by hand.

3 Put all the ingredients into a blender or food processor and whoosh until very smooth. Add salt to taste and whoosh again to mix. Allow to stand for at least an hour before use.

Red pepper coulis

Although it may be used fresh, the flavours will amalgamate and the coulis will improve if kept for a day in the refrigerator. Makes approximately 500 ml of coulis.

3 red peppers

3 plum tomatoes

2 fat red chillies, seeded

1 red onion

50 ml olive oil

250 ml of chicken stock (or water)

100 ml red wine

2 star anise

50 ml grenadine syrup

salt and pepper

1 Preheat your oven to 180°C/350°F/gas mark 4½.

2 Seed and quarter the peppers, and put them in a roasting tin with the tomatoes and chillies. Peel and quarter the red onion and add. Brush with oil and roast for 20 minutes.

3 Put the roasted vegetables, the chicken stock, the wine and the star anise into a saucepan, bring to the boil and cook fiercely until the liquid is reduced by three-quarters.

4 Remove the star anise and purée everything else in a blender or food processor until very smooth. Pass the coulis through a strainer, stir in the grenadine syrup, and adjust the seasoning with salt and pepper.

Simple pasta dough

The basic rule of thumb for pasta is that every diner should get an egg and 100 g of flour! Thus the only variables are how much water and salt to add. The former is governed by the feel of the dough in your hands and the latter by your taste buds (aided by trial and error). This quantity serves four.

400 g Italian, type 00, pasta flour

4 medium eggs

1 heaped teaspoon salt

1 If you have a pasta machine, follow the directions that come with it.

2 Heap the flour on your work surface, make a central well. Then whisk the eggs with the salt and pour into the well. Use a fork to bring the flour into the middle and as soon as possible switch to kneading by hand.

3 Knead for 5 minutes, then rest the dough, wrapped in clingfilm, for 30 minutes.

4 Back to the dough, and knead for another 5 minutes. By now it should feel heavy, smooth and stretchy.

5 Take your longest rolling pin. After flouring it, and the work surface, roll out the dough into a circle. Try to work away from yourself and rotate the piece of dough as you do so. For ravioli, roll out the dough as thinly as possible.

Lentil stew

Serves four.

125 g shallots

2 cloves garlic

75 ml olive oil

350 g Puy lentils

2 bay leaves

750 ml chicken stock (see page 188)

salt and pepper

some good olive oil

some balsamic vinegar

1 Finely chop the shallots, crush the garlic, and cook them both with the olive oil in a heavy saucepan. Do not let them go soft. While they are still crunchy, add the lentils, bay leaves, and the chicken stock. Cover the pan, and simmer as slowly as possible until cooked – between 40 and 60 minutes. Do not overcook as the lentils will turn to mush. Do not season at all during cooking as salt hardens lentils.

2 To finish the lentils, simply season with salt and pepper and stir in a splash of good olive oil and some balsamic vinegar.

Shopping and Showing Off

Puy lentils are the best, but this is a simple dish and any green or brown lentils will suffice. If you cannot buy shallots substitute mild onions.

Home-cured mackerel

Serves eight.

4 mackerel

1 fat red chilli

400 g granulated sugar

200 g sea salt

12 tarragon leaves

6 juniper berries

1 Ask your fishmonger to fillet the mackerel and remove the pin bones.

2 Chop the chilli finely, and add it to the sugar, salt, tarragon and juniper. Mix thoroughly.

3 Put a layer of the mixture in a lidded plastic container, add the fish fillets skin side down,

4 Top with another layer of the mixture, then more fillets, ending with a layer of mixture.

5 Keep in a refrigerator (not too cold!) for 48 hours. The salt mixture will turn to liquid. At the end of the first day turn the fillets over.

6 Before use, rinse the fish well.

Potato, coriander and lemon-grass Dauphinoise

A novel take on the classic Dauphinoise. Serves four.

1 clove garlic

25 g butter

1 kg potatoes

1 bunch fresh coriander (1 × 15 g supermarket pack)

150 g lemon-grass

500 ml whole milk

100 g soft cow's milk cheese

150 g crème fraîche

salt and pepper

1 Preheat your oven to 180°C/350°F/gas mark 4½.

2 Use a large flat gratin dish so that the potato mixture is less than 3 cm deep. Cut the garlic clove in half and rub the dish all over with the cut end. Then butter the dish.

3 Peel the potatoes and slice them very thinly, rinse them in fresh water to get rid of surface starch.

4 Strip the leaves from the coriander and chop finely. Peel the lemon-grass back to the tender middle and chop it very finely.

5 Bring the milk up to the boil in a saucepan. Remove from the heat and stir in the cheese, crème fraîche, coriander and lemon-grass. Then add the potatoes and stir in. Season with salt and pepper.

6 Spoon the contents into the gratin dish, spreading it out evenly into a layer no more than 3 cm thick.

7 Bake in the oven for 80–90 minutes. Brown under the grill to finish, if necessary.

Shopping and Showing off

At Livebait, we use an English cheese called Wellington for this dish, but any soft cow's milk cheese will add the required richness.

Index

index

index